DISCOVERING YOUR TRUE SELF

A GUIDE FOR THE JOURNEY

To Laura Jean —

Celebrating your ordination!

STEVE LANGFORD

Steve Langford

August 2 2010

Ordination Sunday

WESTBOW
PRESS®
A DIVISION OF THOMAS NELSON
& ZONDERVAN

WestBow Press books may be ordered through booksellers or by contacting:

WestBow Press
A Division of Thomas Nelson & Zondervan
1663 Liberty Drive
Bloomington, IN 47403
www.westbowpress.com
1 (866) 928-1240

ISBN: 978-1-9736-9241-6 (sc)
ISBN: 978-1-9736-9240-9 (hc)
ISBN: 978-1-9736-9242-3 (e)

Library of Congress Control Number: 2020909776

Print information available on the last page.

WestBow Press rev. date: 06/12/2020

Also by Steve Langford

Why the Bible Is So Hard to Understand … and Tips to Understanding It

*A God-Shaped World: Exploring Jesus's Teachings about the
Kingdom of God and the Implications for the Church Today*

The Fruit of the Spirit: The Path That Leads to Loving as Jesus Loved

In appreciation for the work of
Richard Blackburn,
Executive Director Emeritus and Senior Consultant,
Lombard Mennonite Peace Center, Lombard, Illinois.

Dedicated to
all who walk the spiritual journey toward
emotional-relational-spiritual maturity.

CONTENTS

INTRODUCTION

Discovering Your True Self is not a book for the casual reader. It is not a book of religious pabulum or of feel-good devotional thoughts. It is a book about a challenging but significantly meaningful and life-transforming journey. It is about a journey that leads us beyond the anxiety and fear that subconsciously dictate our lives. As we make progress on the journey, we break free from anxiety's sabotaging power.

Not only does the journey lead us beyond our default, anxiety-driven ways of thinking and living, it also leads us to discover new, healthier ways of thinking and relating. This journey of discovery leads us to experience life differently. On this journey, we learn to use our power first to manage ourselves and then to make a meaningful difference in the lives of others. It leads us into deeper, more meaningful relationships, into an inner disposition of joy and peace and thanksgiving, and into a joy-filled sense of purpose and meaning. It leads us into greater emotional-relational-spiritual maturity.[1] And it leads us to discover and release our true self.

Your true self may be a new term for many.[2] It may seem foreign and strange. "What do you mean *my true self?* If I am not who I think I am, then who am I? I am just me!"

Even though *your true self* is not a common term in popular discourse, something about it resonates deep within us. We know there is more to who we are than we let other people know. We all have parts of ourselves we hide from even our closest friends and loved ones. We are often aware of an inner *dis*-ease that asks, "Is this all there is to life?"

Thus, the term *your true self* stirs the longing and hope for something more authentic, for something more rewarding and fulfilling, and for something beyond what we have experienced thus far.

This book is a guide to *Discovering Your True Self.* It describes the journey involved. The book falls into three sections. Chapter 1 attempts to communicate my understanding of the journey's goal, *your true self.* Then Part 1 identifies the false self, which is what I call the constructed self. This constructed self is the persona we present to the world. We hide our true self behind it. This persona is an obstacle to discovering our true self. This section shows how anxiety and fear fuel the constructed self and keep it intact. It leads us, step-by-step, to identify the anxiety out of which we live. Recognizing, naming, and managing this anxiety is foundational to the journey. Part 2 focuses on the journey involved in discovering our true self. It identifies what the journey entails and offers concepts, tools, and skills for the journey. Part 3 seeks to describe how life is radically different as we make progress on the journey, moving beyond the anxiety-driven constructed self and beginning to live out of the concepts, tools, and skills that set the true self free.

This study grew out of my life experience. Three streams converged to contribute to this work. The first is my spiritual journey as a follower of Jesus. The heart of this journey is spiritual transformation leading to emotional-relational-spiritual growth. Emotional healing has been an essential dimension of my spiritual journey. My healing involved identifying and facing the fears that controlled my thinking and sabotaged my relationships. The second stream is my journey in recovery as a recovering workaholic. I used my work as a pastor to run from my inner pain, my fear of failure, my fear of intimacy, and my sense of inadequacy as a husband and father. The third contributing stream is my focused study of Bowen Family Systems theory for the past fifteen years. In Bowen Family Systems theory (BFST), I found practical tools for understanding and managing myself. BFST and recovery principles gave me the how-to tools for the inner transformation of my spiritual journey. My journey continues, but I have journeyed far enough to share some of what I have learned. I share it with the prayer my experiences would be signposts for others who would undertake the journey.

So for whom is this book written, if not for the casual reader? It is for those who are aware of a haunting inner dis-ease. It is for those who are afraid of being rejected and left out, afraid of not measuring up and being no good. It is for those who feel inadequate. It is for those who live with fear, anxiety, and worry. It is for those who are lonely. It is for those who punish themselves with self-reproach and self-hate. It is for those who drink from the bitter cup of shame. It is for those who are tired of the nonstop busyness of their lives. It is for those who are weary of the stress of always achieving and competing. It is for those who want something more in their spiritual life than involvement in church activities. It is for those who are tired of trying harder to do better. It is for those who are tired of the pretense and façade. It is for those who are tired of superficial relationships that leave us feeling lonely in a crowd. It is for those who wonder, "Who am I really, deep down inside?" It is for those who want to live with inner peace and joy. It is for those who want something different, something more in their lives. It is for those who want to do something about these things in their lives but don't know where to start. In addition, this book is for those who are already walking the journey.

As *you* walk the journey, I pray this book will be a helpful guide. I pray the principles, truths, and tools that have contributed to my journey will be valuable resources for your journey of *Discovering Your True Self.*

A Guide for Personal Reflection and Journaling, for Group Conversation and Discussion

- What in the preface grabbed you?
- What about the journey appeals to or interests you?
- Why are you reading this book and undertaking the journey?

CHAPTER 1
THE TRUE SELF

The goal of our journey is to discover and live out of our true self.

Who or what is our true self? Our true self is who God created us to be when God knit us together in our mother's womb (Psalm 139:13–14). It is who God originally fashioned us to be. It is who we are as God's handiwork, as God's creation.

Our true self is our unique self. It is who we are that no one else can be. It consists of our gifts and abilities along with our interests and passions. It includes dimensions of our personality, but it is larger than our personality. It includes our strengths and our so-called weaknesses. The true self is tied to the internal aspects of our lives, the realm of attitudes and spirit, principles, and truth. It is who we are deep inside. It is our authentic self.

Our true self never had the opportunity to develop, much less flourish. It was imprisoned in a dungeon by anxiety (as we will see in part 1). It was hidden away, far from the sight of others, to protect it from the assault of shame. It was displaced by a constructed, ego-based self that conformed to what others said we should be if we wanted to be accepted and loved. This constructed, ego-based self is a false self or pseudo self. It is a pretend self.

Thus, the true self has to be discovered and reclaimed. The person God created us to be when we were knit together in our mother's womb has to be released from the dungeon in which is it imprisoned. It has to be set free from the anxiety and shame that keep it locked away.

Our true self is set free to emerge from its hiding place as we grow emotionally-relationally-spiritually. It blossoms as the soul, the divine spark implanted in each of us, is awakened and develops. It is set free as we learn to live beyond the subconscious, sabotaging power of anxiety and fear.

As the true self develops, we live out of an internal sense of personal power and value. We are self-aware and self-responsible. We know how to connect authentically with others and thus do not engage in transactional, merit-based relationships. Comparing and competing are no longer a part of our makeup. We know how to use personal power to be safe. We surrender any effort to control others while trusting God with those things over which we have no control.[3]

As we grow into and live out of our true self, we learn to live with joy and peace and delight. We use power first to manage ourselves and then on behalf of others. Living out of the true self, we use our gifts and abilities to make a difference in the lives of others. We live with egoless self-confidence, relating out of a spirit of confident humility. We are confident in who we are and what we have to offer yet are humble as we recognize all we are and have to offer is the result of God's work in our life (not our achievement through self-effort and willpower). We experience a deep sense of purpose and meaning. We live with openness to all of life and to every person. We experience deep, life-enriching relationships. We live with balance, giving and receiving, doing and being. We live free from the crippling, sabotaging power of anxiety and fear.

Discovering and releasing who God created us to be is the work of the Spirit of God in our lives. It is the Spirit leading us toward the emotional-relational-spiritual maturity.

Thus, there are two dimensions to our true self, both the handiwork of God. The first is who God created us to be when God knit us together in our mother's womb. It is our unique self, the person no one else can ever be. The second dimension is who God is recreating us to be as the Spirit nurtures us toward emotional-relational-spiritual maturity. It is who we are as we mature spiritually.

Discovering our true self involves a journey—a spiritual journey—a journey of transformation—a journey of emotional-relational-spiritual growth— a Spirit-led journey. *Discovering Your True Self* is the essence of life's journey.

A Guide for Personal Reflection and Journaling, for Group Conversation and Discussion

- How familiar are you with the term *true self?* Where did you first hear it?
- What is the meaning, as you understand it, of the term *true self?*
- What did the author's description add to your understanding?
- The author devoted two paragraphs to describing "as the true self develops." What aspect of the description stirs a longing within you?

Our true self is who God created us to be when God knit us together in our mother's womb.

PART 1

THE CONSTRUCTED SELF: HOW ANXIETY AND FEAR SHAPE OUR LIVES

CHAPTER 2
THE GIFT OF FEAR AND ITS DOWNSIDE

The morning sun was just above the horizon, not yet blazing hot as it would be before the end of that summer day. I knelt on my knees in the grass to change a tire that had gone flat the night before as I was cutting wheat. As I worked to loosen the lug nuts on the wheel, a bug buzzed in the grass beside me. I didn't pay much attention to the bug as my focus was on the task before me. But the bug's continued buzzing led me to brush my hand over the grass in an effort to free it and end its incessant buzzing. As I brushed my hand across the grass, I saw what I thought was a bug was actually a rattlesnake coiled and ready to strike. I had knelt down within six inches of its resting place in the grass. Its buzzing was its attempt to warn me I was trespassing on its turf. Instantly, without thinking, I leapt three feet backward, away from the snake. My heart was pounding, my breath rapid, my body shaking. I was wracked with a fear—a fear that had saved me from being bitten by the rattlesnake. My experience of fear was a gift that possibly saved my life that morning.

My rattlesnake experience illustrates my assertion that fear is a gift. It is a survival mechanism designed to protect us from danger.

Fear is the sense of alarm we experience whenever we perceive something or someone as a threat. It is an emotional reaction to danger. The danger may be an actual threat to our well-being, such as the rattlesnake, or something we perceive to be a threat. Whether the danger is real or just perceived, it triggers fear.

Fear launches within us an automatic, subconscious, physical reaction designed to protect us from the danger (i.e., our fear response). I didn't have to take time to analyze the situation with the rattlesnake or think about what response I should make. I reacted automatically, without thinking, to protect myself from the danger. Fear actually bypasses the thinking portion of the brain, communicating directly to the part of the brain that reacts to keep us alive. Thus, our reaction is subconscious, not thought out or consciously chosen.

My reaction was to escape the danger the rattlesnake represented. It was an example of a flight response, the attempt to escape the danger. A fight response would have been to attack the danger in an attempt to eliminate it. A freeze response would have left me frozen and unable to act. These three—flight, fight, and freeze—are the three common automatic, subconscious, physical reactions produced by the experience of fear.

Of course, fear is not unique to us humans. Birds, fish, insects, and other animals all react out of fear. Deer embody the flight response. A badger exemplifies the fight response. A turtle withdrawing into its shell manifests the freeze response. Their ability to experience fear is what helps them stay alive, just as it does us.

The Downside of Fear

In spite of its life-protecting role, fear can have a downside that, rather than protecting us, can work against us. It can enslave us, robbing us of the fullness of life. It has the potential to destroy our health and our relationships. This downside of fear occurs whenever we live with fear, in fear, and out of fear. It is when fear is no longer about a current danger, real or perceived. It is archaic fear—old fear that hangs around haunting our minds. It is fear of *what might be in the future* based upon *what was in the past*. This archaic fear is called anxiety.[4]

We experience anxiety as a nebulous feeling of unease or dis-ease lying just beneath the surface of our awareness. This inner dis-ease is tinged with the feeling of fear associated with a real threat. We are most aware of anxiety when we are in an unfamiliar situation, when we feel out of control, when we do not feel safe, or when we are uncertain of the outcome.[5]

Anxiety is tied to our experiences of fear, especially those associated with our formative years. It is the residue of those previous experiences of fear that still taint our spirit in the present. It is the subconscious memory we carry of those early experiences of being hurt or left out, of being inadequate or treated as *less than* others. Those early experiences taught us to live in anticipation of things in life that would hurt us. They trained us to be on the lookout for what might happen next. The nebulous feeling of unease in our life is this subconscious anticipation of something else that will hurt us. It is the twitching of the old fears. It creates an inner restlessness and a panicky need to do something even though there is no apparent, tangible threat to which to respond. This anxiety, when triggered, gives birth to full blown fear.

> Anxiety is the twitching of old fears.

My experience with the rattlesnake was a graphic, unforgettable experience of fear. It occurred in a specific situation, at a specific time, with a specific danger. Our experience of anxiety is different. It is always present, floating beneath the surface of our awareness. It is the lens through which we see every situation and evaluate every relationship. It is the radar we use to scan the emotional, relational horizon of every group, discerning if the group will be safe or if we will be accepted or if we will have value and standing or if the group will value what we have to offer. Living with anxiety is living on high alert for potential danger.

Living on high alert is costly. While fear is a gift designed to protect us, anxiety can become an inner demon that drives us. Unrecognized and unaddressed, it robs us of peace and joy, setting the emotional tone and inner disposition out of which we live. It shapes our understanding of who we are in relationship to others. It determines how we relate to others as well as how comfortable we are in those relationships. It often undermines our relationships. It determines the triggers of our anger and fears. It determines what we do when we are angry or afraid. It is what lies behind every conflict and broken relationship. It is the driver behind every addiction. It is a factor in every illness.[6] Unrecognized, anxiety has the power to destroy our health, our relationships, and our careers. While fear protects, anxiety sabotages and destroys.

None of us are immune to anxiety and its potentially sabotaging power.

Our experiences of it differ, but each of us carries it with us everywhere we go. It is a part of our emotional DNA.

Living on High Alert

Until we learn to live with self-awareness, our anxiety lies outside our conscious awareness. Yet we are not totally unaware of it. We know it through the inner dis-ease it creates.

Rather than naming and addressing the source of the dis-ease, we generally get trapped in attempting to escape the discomfort the anxiety creates within. Escape strategies differ for each of us.[7]

One strategy almost all of us use is the creation of comfort zones. We create a familiar routine and a comfortable circle of relationships that make us feel safe. We build predictability into our world so that we know what to expect. Our comfort zones help us avoid the unknown and the unexpected. Knowing what to expect translates into a reduced likelihood of anxiety being triggered. Our comfort zones allow us to reduce our anxiety from its high alert status. But our comfort zones are fragile at best. They create a tentative stability rather than true safety. Change is the nature of life. That which is new and different is always disrupting our comfort zones. The unexpected always comes. When the new and different come along, our anxiety creates an automatic resistance to it.

Anxiety is directly tied to our desire to be in control. Thus, another strategy for dealing with anxiety is making to-do lists. To-do lists help us organize our day and focus our energies. They give us a sense of accomplishment as we complete each item and mark items off our list. In other words, they help us feel powerful and in control. To-do lists, while lauded by our production-oriented culture, are often a mask for unrecognized anxiety about being inadequate and out of control. Similarly, the drive to achieve or produce is another way we attempt to numb anxiety.

Another strategy most of us use is some habit or activity to numb the pain of our anxiety. I poured myself into my work, becoming a workaholic, in an effort to numb the deep-seated fear that haunted my inner being. We all know how people turn to alcohol, drugs, smoking, and prescription medications in an effort to numb the pain. Others turn to busyness, computer games, food, smoking, gambling, nonstop talking, partying, pornography, sex, or hoarding. Teens often engage in cutting or starving themselves when these other patterns can't contain the pain of the anxiety. In reality, almost anything *done in excess* can become a way of escaping the inner disease: being with people, eating, exercise, sports, running, entertainment, hobbies, religion, busyness, shopping, etc.

Comfort zones, to-do lists, and addictive patterns are not the only ways of dealing with the pain anxiety produces. Some seek to avoid anxiety and its pain by controlling others and the situations they face. Others internalize the anxiety, pushing it down into their bodies where it produces physical illnesses. In doing so, these individuals command their family's focus and, with it, the anxiety within the family system. The family's focus, in turn, reduces or binds the family's level of anxiety. It is as though the one person's illness carries the anxiety of the larger family. Parents often pour their lives into their children, making their children the focus of their existence. This overfocus transfers the parents' anxiety onto the child. This transferred anxiety has the power to impair the child.[8] Another more acceptable means of coping is helping. Anxiety pushes some to become involved in another's problems, attempting to fix them. The other person's struggle and pain stir anxiety in the helper. The helper's way of reducing their own anxiety is to fix the other's problem.[9] Emotional distance— living emotionally walled off from others—is a common coping mechanism used particularly, but not exclusively, by men.

Some, rather than seeking to escape the inner dis-ease, live out of it. They externalize it. They allow their anxiety to invade life, dumping it on whatever is going on and whoever is around. They are emotionally reactive, emotionally expressive people. When their anxiety is triggered, fear takes over, dominating their thinking. They become emotionally out of control, allowing the emotion to drive them. Some of us become consumed with worry.[10] Some of us externalize our anxiety by attacking others with it. We criticize, judge, find fault, and blame. Drama queens live in a never-ending cycle of emotional drama. They move from one emotionally charged experience to another. They become addicted to the drama and the adrenaline the drama produces. Their paths are littered with conflict and broken relationships, the product of unrecognized and unmanaged anxiety.

Whatever the strategy, the objective is the same: to deal with the uneasiness deep within, without having to face it, name it, and address it.

A Better Way

The good news is there is another, better way of dealing with anxiety, one that can set us free from anxiety's destructive, sabotaging power and control. It is a better way, but not an easy way. This better way is foundational to *Discovering Your True Self.*

My experience of fear of the rattlesnake bypassed my thinking. I automatically reacted. Moving beyond the sabotaging power of anxiety requires us to *engage* the thinking portion of our brains. It involves recognizing, naming, and learning to manage the old fears. It involves recognizing and moving beyond the old, unhealthy patterns we use to numb the pain of the anxiety. It involves moving through the old pain to inner healing. It involves trained self-awareness. It is a journey into emotional-relational-spiritual maturity. Such is the journey of *Discovering Your True Self.*

A Guide for Personal Reflection and Journaling, for Group Conversation and Discussion

- Relate a personal experience of fear similar to the author's experience with the rattlesnake.
- The author described *anxiety* as archaic or old fear. What would you add to his description?
- Where do you recognize anxiety in your life?
- What reaction does the term *living on high alert* stir within you?
- What strategies do you use to manage anxiety in your life?

CHAPTER 3
SET FREE: THE STORY OF
A TORMENTED SOUL

The book of Mark in the Christian scriptures relates a healing story that provides us guidance for our journey beyond the destructive, sabotaging power of fear and anxiety.[11]

Jesus and his disciples had crossed the Sea of Galilee, leaving the western, Jewish shore to go to the eastern shore in Gentile territory. As they stepped out of the boat, Jesus was confronted by a man described as being possessed by an unclean spirit. The writer's description of the man is of a tortured soul. He lived in the ravine caves that served as tombs for the region. He was constantly howling and hurting himself with stones. The local people viewed him as dangerous to himself and others. They had attempted to control him but had been unable to do so. He had broken free from every restraint they had used.

This tormented man confronted Jesus as he stepped out of the boat. "What have you to do with me, Jesus, Son of the Most High God? I adjure you by God, do not torment me."[12] In the dialogue that took place, an interesting detail is noted: Jesus was unable to cast out the unclean spirit! The word used in verse 8, in the original Greek, expresses the idea of repeated attempts: "he had been saying to him." Jesus had repeatedly commanded the unclean spirit to leave the man, but the spirit refused to obey. Faced with an impasse, Jesus changed tactics. Putting aside direct confrontation, Jesus asked the man, "What is your name?" The man responded, "My name is Legion;[13] for we are many." The man's response was as though the unclean spirit was speaking. "I am a broken, fragmented man. There are so many parts of me; I have no single, unifying identity. I am Legion, the broken man." At that point, the impasse was overcome. The unclean spirit begged Jesus to allow them to leave the man and enter a herd of pigs feeding nearby. Jesus granted them permission, resulting in the man's healing.

The turning point in this story of healing was when the man (the unclean spirit) named his condition. "My name is Legion; for we are many."

The unknown is always frightening. In facing the unknown, we often anticipate the worse. This tendency is called catastrophic thinking. Knowing what we are facing often reduces our sense of fear of it. More than one person has said, "At least now we know what we are dealing with." As long as that which we face is unknown, it has power over us. Giving it a name breaks its power.

Naming our fear breaks the power it holds over us.

A Guide for Personal Reflection and Journaling, for Group Conversation and Discussion

- To what part of the story do you relate?
- When have you experienced a sense of relief by naming the unknown?

CHAPTER 4
NAMING OUR FEARS

In order to name our fears, we first must understand the life forces and basic emotional needs that shape us. These life forces and emotional needs are what give birth to our fears.

Togetherness and Individuality: Life's Emotional Seesaw

We humans, along with all biological life-forms, are influenced by two emotional life forces. One is a *togetherness* force, the desire to connect with others like me. This life force translates into our pursuit of security. "There is safety in numbers" expresses this pursuit. The other life force is an *individuality* force, the desire to be my own, separate self. This life force translates into the pursuit of our own identity separate from the group. Obviously, these two life forces are at odds with one another. The one leads us toward togetherness; the other, toward separateness.[14]

Every person lives with the tension created by these two opposing life forces. We all desire the gifts they offer: being a part of a group and being one's own individual self. But by nature, each of us is more inclined to one over the other.

Those of us who live more out of the togetherness force are willing to sacrifice our individuality in order to belong. We live by the motto "Go along to get along." In a group, we take on the thinking, values, and positions of the group. In a personal relationship, we adapt to the other, seldom challenging the thinking or position of the other person in the relationship. We surrender self, giving up much of who we are, in order to belong.

Those of us who live more out of the individuality force are willing to sacrifice our place in the large group in order to maintain our own individuality. We are willing to sacrifice belonging in order to be "my own self."

Every relationship involves an ongoing struggle to balance these two life forces. Like a seesaw, the relationship shifts from one side of the togetherness-individuality continuum to the other. When the relationship has too much togetherness for one person's comfort level, that person acts in a way to shift the balance toward the individuality side. Anger and conflict, which create emotional distance in the relationship, are often used to create this kind of shift. When the relationship has too much separateness for one or the other's comfort level, that one acts in a way to shift the balance toward the togetherness side.[15] Children playing on a seesaw, each pushing off the ground to make the other go down, illustrate this dynamic in a relationship.

Emotional Needs: The Soil from Which Our Fears Grow

These two life forces and the gifts they offer translate into four basic emotional needs. Two of these needs relate to the togetherness force, two to the individuality force. The togetherness life force and the security it promises translate into a need to be safe and a need to belong. The security we pursue is rooted in the need to feel safe within a relationship or group. The individuality life force and the separateness it promotes translate into a need to have a sense of power or ability along with a need to have a sense of significance and value.[16]

Togetherness		Individuality
Security	▲	Identity
the need to be safe		the need to have power or ability
the need to belong		the need to have value, significance

We were created for relationship (i.e., the need to belong). The desire to connect with another or a group is a part of our emotional makeup. The experience of loneliness grows out of this need. But we cannot truly connect with another (i.e., belong) if we do not feel safe in the relationship. Feeling safe is a prerequisite to belonging. Safeness may be the foundational need. This need to be safe gives birth to our innate fear response.

The desire to have our own individuality, separate from others, is also a part of our emotional makeup. Our individuality and sense of identity are tied to what we can do (i.e., power and ability). Our abilities are part of what make us unique and set us apart. They are what we have to offer to a relationship or to a group. They are the gifts we have to give. They are also what give us a sense of value or significance. They are the means by which we gain place or standing in a group. We cannot truly belong, much less have significance or standing in the group, if the group does not value who we are or what we have to offer.

The interrelatedness of these four needs is seen in the experience of schoolchildren choosing up sides at recess. The order of selection is based upon ability for the game to be played. The strongest, the fastest, the biggest, the most coordinated, or most popular are chosen first. Then the strongest, the fastest, the biggest, the most coordinated of those who haven't been chosen are picked next. The process of choosing continues until there is but one kid left. That kid is not really chosen. He is assigned to a team because he is not really wanted. He is viewed as having nothing of significance to offer the team. This choosing of sides touches on all four emotional needs: the need to be safe, to belong, to have power and ability, and to have value. Apart from being valued, there is no belonging or safeness. The last kid chosen doesn't really belong because what he has to offer is not really valued.

We all live with these four emotional needs. We all long for a safe place to belong in which who we are and what we can do (ability) is valued. Our closest relationships (i.e., friendships and love relationships), are with those with whom we feel safe and connected because they value who we are and what we can do.

Our fears and anxieties are rooted in these four basic emotional needs. These emotional needs are the soil from which our fears grow. Identifying and understanding these four basic emotional needs puts us in a position to name our fear.

Four Deep-seated Fears

Each of these four basic emotional needs has a twin, so to speak. It has a flip side, a corresponding deep-seated fear. We fear what we would experience if these basic needs were not met.

The need to be safe carries with it the fear of *being hurt*. The need to belong carries the fear of *being left out, rejected, or abandoned*. The need for a sense of power or ability gives birth to the *fear of being inadequate, incapable, weak, or powerless*.[17] The need for a sense of value or significance carries the *fear of being insignificant, less than, or no good*. The desire for respect is an expression of this need and its fear.

Togetherness		Individuality
Security	▲	Identity

Safeness — *hurt*	Power & ability — *inadequate*
Belonging — *left out, abandoned, rejected*	Value & significance — *less than*

Because we all live with these four basic emotional needs, we all also know their corresponding fears. We have known what it is like to be hurt (physically, emotionally, verbally, intellectually, or sexually). We have known the pain of being left out, rejected, and abandoned. We have known the pain of not measuring up, leaving us feeling inadequate, incapable, weak, or powerless. We have known the pain of feeling less important than another or insignificant or no good. And we know the fear of experiencing such pain again.

The anxiety with which we live is the subconscious fear we will experience these pains yet again. We live on high alert so that we might avoid ever experiencing that kind of pain again. In addition to wanting to avoid such pain again, anxiety's power is tied to a deep-seated fear that we *are* the very thing we fear. We want to avoid experiencing the pain again because the experience validates our deep fear: we are powerless and will be hurt, we are unwanted and will be rejected, we are inadequate (flawed) and won't measure up, and we are no good and have no real value.

A Guide for Personal Reflection and Journaling, for Group Conversation and Discussion

- Identify an occasion when you have experienced the pull of the togetherness force. Identify an occasion when you have experienced the pull of the individuality force.
- Identify on which side of the continuum you commonly fall: togetherness or individuality. Remember you desire the gifts offered by both sides of the continuum but naturally lean to one or the other.
- Relate a personal experience from your childhood of each of the four basic needs: need to be safe, need to belong, need to have a sense of power and ability, and need to have a sense of value.
- Relate a personal experience from your childhood of each of the four fears: being hurt, being rejected, being inadequate and not measuring up, and being less than or insignificant.
- What feelings stir as you remember your early experiences?
- Identify when you have experienced these fears as an adult.

CHAPTER 5

THE LAND OF THE GIANTS: THE BREEDING GROUND FOR ANXIETY

The anxiety with which we live is tied to memories of previous experiences of emotional pain. We subconsciously live in fear of experiencing such pain again. Our fear is the aftermath of our earliest experiences of pain. It is old fear rooted in the past. Yet even though it is old, it is very much alive and present, floating just beneath the surface of our awareness as *anxiety*.

Those early experiences of pain and the fear they stirred are primarily rooted in our formative years, when we lived in the land of giants. At this stage of our lives, giants (adults) dominated our world. The giants were huge and seemingly all-powerful. We were small and powerless by comparison. Because we were no taller than their knees, we had to look up to see their faces. Thankfully, most of the giants were kind and caring—most of the time. We could depend on them to meet our needs. They met our physical needs. They fed us, clothed us, bathed us, and put us to bed. In addition, they met our emotional needs. They helped us, taught us, held us, and hugged us. They comforted us when we were hurt. We felt safe with them and loved (valued) by them. Their caring helped us feel like we belonged, even though we were not giants.

But there were times, particularly as we explored and experimented with our own power, we incurred the displeasure of the giants. We said or did things they disliked. Sometimes, they corrected us with kindness and understanding, but other times, they were irritated and put out by what we did. In those instances, they were not as kind and understanding. They were angry and often loud.

My description of these early experiences is not to blame the giants (i.e., our parents, extended family, caregivers, and teachers). The description is an attempt to paint a picture from the perspective of a preschooler. The experiences I describe are a normal part of growing up. Everyone experienced them in some form or another. Some giants were better at helping us learn and develop than others. Others struggled to help us because they were too overwhelmed with responsibility, were too exhausted, did not know how to be a parent, or were too emotionally immature and wounded. These realities are a fact of life.

In addition to their size and power, the giants had another advantage over us: they could think. During this stage of our development, our abilities to think and use reason were not developed. Those abilities, located in the cerebral cortex, do not even begin to develop until the age of four or five. This part of the brain does not mature until we become giants ourselves, sometime between the age of twenty-five and thirty. So we could not understand what was happening in our world. Even if a giant tried to explain what was happening (which most never did), we could not understand it.

My wife and I went through a move associated with a job change when our oldest two boys were four and two. We talked with our boys about the upcoming move, about packing our things in boxes, about loading the boxes on a truck, and about moving to a different house in a different state. We thought we had prepared our boys for the upcoming move. Several weeks after we had relocated and were settled into our new house in a new city, our oldest son came to his mother and said, "Okay. We moved. Now let's go home." He had understood what we had said about the move, but he did not understand the move was not for a short time like our family vacations.

As young children living in the land of the giants, we did not have the intellectual ability to understand what we were experiencing. But we could sense the emotions the giants were experiencing in the event. We could read them emotionally. Their emotions left an imprint on us beyond our conscious awareness.

Other factors impacted our life in the land of giants. Younger siblings came along to invade our world and claim the giants' attention and affection. Older siblings were jealous that we invaded their world. They viewed us as competitors. Or they claimed us as their own, taking control of our lives and telling us what to do. We younger siblings were always trying to keep up with the older ones, doing what they did. But we could never do what they did as well as they did it. They had the unfair advantage of being older, but we didn't understand that. Sometimes events happened that disturbed the family: an illness, a death, a move, the loss of a job, a divorce, a crisis in the community, etc. We didn't understand what was happening, but we felt it. We felt the fear, anxiety, angst, and anger the giants felt. We sensed their anxiety.

Our experiences in the land of the giants were often reinforced during our school years. Kids have an amazing ability to know just what to say to play on our fears. "You're not my friend anymore" plays on the need to belong. "You're fat (or dumb or stupid)" touches the need for a sense of power and ability. "Ewww. You're disgusting" attacks the need for a sense of value and significance. And then there were the bullies! These kinds of comments often made our kid-dominated world an unsafe place emotionally.

Most of our memories from our time in the land of the giants are not conscious memories. (Remember the cerebral cortex was not developed.) Rather, they are emotional memories stored in a part of the brain associated with survival instincts.[18] Those events that stirred pain left an imprint. While we may not remember the details of the event (a function of the cerebral cortex), we do remember the pain and the fear it stirred. We live with the emotional memory. *Those emotional memories are the fuel of our anxiety.* They are our emotional default setting.

Anxiety is the fear we will again experience the pain we experienced before. It is the fear of once again being hurt or rejected, of being powerless and inadequate, of being insignificant and less than another. Our experiences from our school years, particularly those that touched these deep-seated fears, reinforced these emotional memories from the land of the giants and fed the anxiety.

Anxiety-Shaped Patterns

The land of the giants was the breeding ground of the anxiety with which we live as adults. In addition, how we coped with anxiety was developed in the land of the giants. These patterns helped us to survive in the midst of anxiety filled experiences.

Our experience in the land of the giants trained us to focus on others, training us to react to what others did. Learning to read the giants' emotions was how we survived. We sensed when they were pleased or when they were angry, when they were at

> The land of the giants was the breeding ground of the anxiety with which we live as adults.

peace, or when they were upset and anxious. We didn't always understand why they were angry, but we learned to be afraid of them when they were. We learned how to avoid them and their anger.

This focus on others led to our efforts to control the other. We quickly learned to do those things that pleased the giants and to avoid those things that angered them. In doing so, we were seeking to control what they thought about us and how they reacted to us.

These efforts to control the giants were different for each of us, built around our innate personality and strengths. Those of us who are naturally gregarious and outgoing learned to entertain the giants and make them laugh. Those of us who are more introverted learned to withdraw and avoid. Some of us went so far as to be invisible. Others of us learned to use our abilities to achieve and perform, gaining the giants' approval. Others of us learned to be helpful, taking on responsibilities and tasks far beyond our chronological age. We took care of younger siblings or household chores. We became Daddy's little helper. We developed these patterns in an effort to gain attention, acceptance, approval, applause, affirmation, and affection. Who of us hasn't heard a child calling out to a parent, "Watch me, Mommy! Watch me!"? Some of us used our abilities to manipulate the giants. We learned if Momma said no, Daddy would say yes or vice versa. Others of us learned to use our anger to get what we wanted as most giants don't know how to deal with the battle of wills embodied in temper tantrums. Some of us adopted an attitude of defiance and rebellion, being willing to endure the consequences. More than a few of us stopped trying. Others of us found a way to escape the home.

We developed these patterns as a way of dealing with our anxiety. We created them in our effort to be safe and to belong, to have a sense of power and value. They were our attempt to get the giants to meet our basic emotional needs. They were (and are!) our emotional survival mechanisms.

We eventually outgrew the land of the giants as we grew into giants (adults) ourselves. But we did not leave the land of the giants behind. We carried our experiences in the land of the giants with us in the form of anxiety. We also carried the patterns we developed during those years:

- our focus on others
- our sensitivity to the emotional disposition of the other
- our attempts to control what the other thought about us and how they related to us
- our attempts to get our needs met through others.

While these patterns helped us to survive in the land of the giants, they become detrimental when we become one of the giants. The anxiety and these survival-oriented patterns are residue from the land of the giants that undermine our emotional health as adults and become a barrier to healthy relationships.

A Guide for Personal Reflection and Journaling, for Group Conversation and Discussion

- Identify some of the factors from your formative years that shaped who you are and the anxiety with which you live.
- What negative messages from your childhood can you still hear in your mind?
- This chapter identified four patterns we developed during our formative years: focus on others, sensitivity to the other's emotional disposition, attempt to control what the other thought about us and how they related to us, and attempt to get our emotional

needs met by the other. Identify an experience of each of these four patterns during your childhood years.

- Where do you see these patterns at play in your life today?
- What method did you adopt in order to deal with anxiety in the land of the giants? What was your survival strategy?

CHAPTER 6

IN THE GRIP OF FEAR: THE FEAR THAT DRIVES US

The journey of *Discovering Your True Self* involves identifying and addressing both the anxiety and the patterns we developed in the land of the giants. Our next step on the journey is to name the specific fear that drives us. What is the face of the anxiety that governs my life?

We all live with the four basic emotional needs and their corresponding fears. Of those four, however, one overshadows the others. That one need is what is most important to us emotionally. It is our *primary emotional need*. Along with this primary need is its corresponding fear. This one fear is what we dread the most. It is our *dominant fear*. It is what drives us.

Our primary need and dominant fear do not mean the other three needs are not important to us or the other corresponding fears do not affect us. Rather, we function out of the assumption if this primary need is met, then the other three needs will be met as well. If we can avoid this one fear, then all will be well in our lives.[19] As a result, we use our power to get our primary need met and to avoid the fear that drives our lives. Underlying our efforts is the anxiety we will once again experience the pain of this driving fear.

I speak of this one fear as our driving fear because of the power it wields in our lives. Consider its impact. It is the power behind the anxiety with which we live. It sets the emotional tone and inner disposition out of which we live. It becomes the foundation of our identity, shaping our sense of self. It dictates how we function in relationships (our relational pattern) and how comfortable we are in relationships. Our driving fear is the trigger to our hot buttons and creates the pattern with which we react when our buttons are pushed. It is the underlying issue in every conflict. In short, our dominant, driving fear is the central emotional issue of our life.[20]

The following chapters explore the specifics of how this dominant fear impacts us. Exploring these subconscious aspects of our emotional life will help us become more aware of them, putting us in a position to manage them. Such awareness is the doorway to growth and change. It is a necessary tool on the journey to *Discovering Your True Self.*

A Guide for Personal Reflection and Journaling, for Group Conversation and Discussion

- Reflect again on the four basic needs and their corresponding fears identified in chapter 3. Which do you identify as your primary need? Your dominant fear?
- What old messages still play in your mind, reflecting and reinforcing this driving fear?

CHAPTER 7
RESIDUE FROM THE LAND OF THE GIANTS: A FEAR-BASED IDENTITY

When we left the land of the giants, we carried with us the anxiety developed there along with the patterns we developed to deal with that anxiety. The two primary patterns we developed were a focus on others and our attempts to use our power to control what those others thought and did. These two patterns, fueled by our dominant fear, impact us at the very core of our being: our identity.

As children, we learned to see ourselves through the eyes of others. How the giants viewed and treated us shaped how we saw ourselves. We were trained to tie our sense of who we are to the thinking, emotions, and reactions of others. We tied our sense of identity to something *outside* of ourselves.

> We were trained to tie our sense of who we are to the thinking, emotions, and reactions of others ... to something outside of ourselves.

Our primary need and dominant fear point to the identity we developed through the influence of key people in our formative years.

When our primary need is to be *safe*, our driving fear is of being hurt. Consequently, we hide ourselves from others. We build walls to keep people at a safe distance. Only a small, select few are allowed to get close, but even those relationships are managed with emotional distance. We do not allow them to get close or really know us. Our sense of identity is

29

hidden away, overshadowed by our fear of being hurt. We often do not even know ourselves. All we know is our fear. Behind the fear is a sense of being small and powerless.

When our primary need is *belonging*, our driving fear is of being rejected or abandoned. Consequently, we tie our sense of self to another, either an individual or a group. We adapt to the thinking, desires, and needs of the other, surrendering who we are in exchange for acceptance. We use our power to help, to take care of, and to make and keep others happy. We grant the other the power to determine our value (identity). We have no value apart from being in a relationship.

When our primary need is *power*, our driving fear is of being inadequate or incapable, weak or powerless. We live with the fear of not measuring up. Consequently, we tie our sense of self to our abilities, particularly to our accomplishments as indicators of our ability. We avoid anything that might suggest we are in any way inadequate. We find an area of life in which we excel and have the appearance of being an authority. We like to be in charge. We often think of ourselves as knowing more than others. Any experience of failure can be devastating to us as it validates our greatest fear: being inadequate and incapable.

When our primary need is *value*, our driving fear is of being insignificant or less than another. We live with the fear of having no value. Consequently, we tie our sense of self to having significance and standing with a group. Our driving fear leads us to equate our value (identity) with being recognized, respected, loved, and appreciated by others. Our sense of self is often tied to a position we hold or a role we play or a title we carry. When our sense of value is tied to something outside ourselves, we use our power to prove our value through what we do. Any experience of feeling devalued or disrespected can undo us emotionally. We can also tie our sense of self to an individual. Our value is linked to being loved by someone of the opposite sex (or same sex, if we are LGBTQ+). This inclination lies behind the teenage practice of "going steady" and other early love relationships.

Sometimes our driving fear is overwhelming. In such situations, we surrender to the fear, living as though what we fear most is true about us. We surrender to the fear of being hurt, retreating from life and people (need to be safe). Because of our fear of being rejected or abandoned, we tolerate abusive relationships and situations. We live as the black sheep of the family or as rebels against the status quo. When we surrender to our fear of not measuring up and being inadequate, we live below our potential, underfunctioning rather than developing and maximizing our abilities. We underachieve and underperform as though we were failures with nothing to offer. The fear of having no value or standing leads us to live as if we are no-good nobodies. We live with no self-respect and expect no respect from others.

Again, we may experience any or all of these fears at one time or another, but one will be dominant. We subconsciously believe if we can avoid this one thing we fear, then everything will be all right. We believe if this one need is met, the other three needs would be met too.

The driving power of these fears is reinforced by old messages from the world in which we grew up. Generally these messages were communicated verbally but they were also communicated through the way we were treated. We were told the world was not a safe place and people would hurt us. We were taught to play our cards close to the vest, to not call attention to ourselves, and to blend in with the wallpaper. We were told to never take unnecessary risks or trust anyone. These messages reinforce our fear of being hurt. We were told we were unlovable and no one would ever like us, much less want us or love us. Others made fun of us, communicating something about us was unacceptable. We learned to fear and avoid conflict, to not make waves, and to let sleeping dogs lie. These messages reinforce our fear of rejection and abandonment. We were told we were flawed: dumb, fat, stupid, ugly, etc. We were repeatedly criticized. Nothing we did was ever good enough. We were led to believe we couldn't do anything right and would never amount to anything. These messages reinforce our fear of being inadequate and incapable. We were compared to a brother or sister and told we could not do _____ as well as they could. What we thought was ridiculed or ignored. What someone else wanted always took priority over what we wanted. These messages reinforce our fear of being insignificant and less than.

Part of the power of these driving fears lies in the deep-seated, subconscious fear the old messages are true. We live in fear we *are* unlovable and will be rejected, we *are* inadequate and incapable, we *are* insignificant and less than and so we *will* be hurt. These fears are like the monster under the bed: no one can see them, but we know they are there. We are driven to escape them. We live in constant awareness of anything that might validate them. In other words, we live on high alert with deep-seated anxiety.

Of course, not all of the messages with which we grew up were negative. Some of us grew up with the sense of being special: Mom's/Dad's/Grandma's favorite, the prince or princess, the talented one, the smart one, the athlete, the name bearer, the hero. The firstborn, the only child, the first boy, the first girl, the baby—anyone who occupied one of these family positions generally lives with a sense of place (belonging) and standing (value) in the family. That place and standing are never in question (safe). They often have a voice (power) other siblings do not have. Yet even these seemingly positive messages can carry a negative dimension. They often carry a burden along with the privilege. Expectations are generally attached to them. There is a price to pay for being the special one in a family or organization.

Our driving fear leads us to tie our sense of self to something outside of ourselves. The response of others is a major player in how we see ourselves. This outside focus grants people power over us—a power we give them!

As was true in the land of the giants, our driving fear keeps our focus on others. This focus on others and their reactions blinds us to who we were created to be. It keeps our focus on externals, blinding us to the interior realm. The interior realm is the true realm of identity and the key to belonging. The interior realm is the realm of gifts and abilities, of passions, and of values and principles. These qualities define who we really are (i.e., our true self) and are the basis for genuine connection with others.

Our journey of *Discovering Your True Self* leads us to a new identity. That identity is a dimension of our true self, the person God created us to be.

A Guide for Personal Reflection and Journaling, for Group Conversation and Discussion

- In which description(s) do you see something of yourself?
- Identify the feelings these descriptions stir.

- Which old message(s) did you hear as you grew up?
- Which ones play in your head today?
- Identify the old messages you repeat to yourself. When do you repeat them to yourself?

CHAPTER 8

RESIDUE FROM THE LAND OF THE GIANTS: HOW FEAR SHAPES OUR RELATIONSHIPS

Our journey in the land of the giants not only trained us to focus on others, it also trained us to attempt to control them. We learned to believe (incorrectly) we were responsible for what they felt and, consequently, what they thought about us. We believed (incorrectly) we could make the giants happy or angry. We believed (incorrectly) we could get them to do what we wanted. Although they were physically bigger and stronger than us, we believed (incorrectly) we could control them emotionally. How we live in relationship with others today (i.e., our relational pattern) is shaped by this pattern of attempting to control what others think, feel, and do. We continue to follow the faulty thinking that we can do so. And of course, our efforts are fueled by anxiety.

Recognizing Our Relational Pattern

Our relational pattern is determined by how we use our power in relationships. All of us inherently use our power to assure our primary emotional need will be met and our dominant, driving fear will be avoided.

When we are driven by our *fear of being hurt,* we use our power to control. We seek to control others. We seek to control the situation. We use our power to build walls to keep other people at a safe distance emotionally. We use our power to hide. We hide in work, in silence, in incessant talking, in humor, in busyness,

> Our relational pattern is determined by how we use our power in relationships.

in physical absence, or in anything that will keep people at a safe distance.[21]

Molly is a strong personality who runs a tight ship.[22] She is heavily involved in her children's lives, monitoring their busy schedules and getting everyone to where they are supposed to be, when they are supposed to be there. Homework is done under her supervising eye. Each child has specific chores to which they are assigned with expected deadlines for completion. Her husband lets her call the shots and set the agenda. Molly has little involvement outside of her kids' lives. Her circle of trusted friends is small. Even within that small group, she shares little of herself and her history. She primarily talks about her kids and their activities. Molly has created a small world, built around her family, where she feels in control and safe from the rest of the world. She lives with the incessant anxiety something will disrupt their lives, bringing chaos and pain to her ordered world. Molly is driven by her need to feel safe. She lives in fear of being hurt.

Mary is also driven by the fear of being hurt. But instead of using her power to protect herself by controlling, Mary abdicates her power. She is a worrier who worries about everything. She lives as a modern-day hermit who is isolated and cut off from others. Even her contact with her family is limited. She loses herself in the fantasies found in romantic novels and soap operas on TV. She hoards things, filling her physical surroundings to offset the emptiness of her inner life. She concentrates her power in some obsession, such as organizing her personal belongings or repeatedly washing her hands to ensure they are clean.

When we are driven by the *fear of being left out, rejected, or abandoned*, we use our power to take care of others. Our focus is always on the other. Our radar is constantly scanning to identify what the other needs, what the other wants, what the other feels, or what the other's mood is. Assuming we have the power to make the other person happy and thus control how they feel about us (we don't), we work to keep the other happy. We seek to meet their needs and fulfill their desires. We sacrifice ourselves to do so.

We give up what we think, ignore how we feel, and deny what we need in order to cater to the other's needs and desires. In our minds, the other people and their needs are more important than we are. This perception is tied to others' power to reject and abandon us. This driving fear of being rejected leads us to avoid confrontation and conflict at any cost. We live without clear boundaries.[23] We are helpers, caretakers, givers, and people pleasers. We often end up in abusive relationships in which the other—spouse, friend, church, social group, or workplace—take advantage of us. We often endure such relationships while wearing a "happy face."[24]

Debra is an outgoing, caring person whose smile can melt a negative mood in a heartbeat. She is always upbeat and positive. She is a giving person who is always taking care of others. She can always be depended upon to respond to any need when it surfaces. She sacrifices herself, spending enormous time and energy in helping others. She is the casserole and dessert queen of her neighborhood and church, always showing up with one or the other (or both!) when misfortune strikes. She does not know the meaning of no when it comes to helping others. She is uncomfortable when others are upset and swiftly acts to comfort them. At any social event, she is serving food and providing drinks rather than engaging in social interactions with other guests. She prefers to help serve rather than be served. She is a devoted wife who is attentive to her husband's every need and desire. She is quick to apologize and make amends if he is upset or unhappy. She never complains or says a cross word. Debra lives with the nagging anxiety she will do something to anger and offend someone. She is driven by the need to belong. She lives in fear of being rejected.

Diana is also driven by the fear of being rejected and abandoned. But she, like Mary, has abdicated her power, living as though she were powerless. She lives in a loveless, abusive marriage to an alcoholic. She is a codependent who enables her husband's alcoholism. Unlike Debra, Diana does complain. She frequently nags her husband about his drinking but to no avail. He ignores her nagging by numbing himself with yet another six-pack of beer. Diana tolerates a loveless, abusive relationship because of her fear of being alone. Being alone means she is unlovable and has been rejected. So Diana lives as though she has no power, a victim of her situation. Her emotional payoff for living in such a relationship is her sense of moral superiority to her alcoholic husband. She may be unlovable, but she is not the kind of person he is. She is better than that.

When we are driven by the *fear of being inadequate and incapable, weak and powerless*, we use our power to demonstrate how powerful we are. Our abilities are always on display. Consequently, we are always in performance mode. We are strong personalities who generally take charge. We have strong opinions and are quick to assert them, demonstrating our great depth of knowledge. We talk more than we listen. We dominate conversations and groups. We are achievers and overachievers. We take pride in doing things right and on schedule. We wear the mantel of achievement and success. The way we dress speaks of our achievement. We are generally impatient, intolerant, and condescending toward those who are not as competent. Our identity is tied to being better than others: stronger, smarter, and more successful. We do things right.

Brad is a beneficent dictator. As a dictator, he calls the shots in every sphere of his life. He operates with the confidence he is right and his way is best. He is always in control. As a beneficent dictator, his controlling personality is tempered by a caring, helpful veneer. Others respect him and appreciate what he does for them. They enjoy the gifts he doles out. They defer to him and his leadership. Brad lives with the anxiety someone will see beneath his veneer of strength. He is driven by the need for power and ability. He lives in fear of not measuring up as failure would reveal his inadequacy, lack of capability, weakness, and powerlessness.

Bill is also driven by the fear of being inadequate, incapable, weak, and powerless. But Bill, like Mary and Diana, abdicates his power. He has surrendered to the old messages that he is a waste of space who can never do anything right. Believing he has no skills to offer, Bill drifts from one low-paying job to another. He drowns out his pain with alcohol and drugs. He is an angry man. He is an avid fan of his favorite football and hockey team, feeling great when they win and criticizing and complaining when they lose. He is quick to criticize referees and others in authority roles. He often rants about select groups he views as worthless and no good, complaining about "those filthy _____." He is likely married to someone like Diana.

When we are driven by the *fear of being insignificant or less than*, we use our power to prove our worth and value. We push ourselves to excel because anything less than excellence would make us less than those who did excel. We too are achievers and overachievers, helpers and givers. We generally go the extra mile in our work, church, and social relationships. Our efforts bring us attention and appreciation. We enjoy positions of leadership and influence. Our identity is tied to being recognized, appreciated, respected, and valued. Being slighted, overlooked, ridiculed, or rejected is not just painful; it is debilitating.

Victor is an intense person who has spent his life striving to achieve. Yet no accomplishment is satisfying for long. Something else, something more, captures his attention and he is off in pursuit of his next achievement. He overfunctions, doing more than is necessary, taking on responsibilities that belong to others. He tends to be a perfectionist, wanting to do everything with excellence. Adequate is not acceptable. Failure is unthinkable. Because he is dependable, he is often placed in positions of leadership and responsibility. What other people think of him is important. He spends much of his energy in trying to gain and keep the respect and appreciation of others. Victor operates out of *if... then* thinking, assuming that proving his worth will bring respect and guarantee acceptance (belonging). Being accepted and valued, in his mind, means he will not be hurt (safeness). Victor lives with an unacknowledged anxiety that he is really no good. He is driven by the need to be valued. He lives in fear of being insignificant and unimportant.

Victoria is also driven by the fear of being insignificant, but she too has abdicated her power. She lives as though she has nothing of value to offer even though others often affirm her abilities. She seldom gets involved in any group. When she does, she lives on the fringes. She constantly compares herself with others who can do what she can't. She interprets their ability as evidence she is no good. "I try to ..." and "I wish I could ..." are phrases she uses often. Truth be told, she doesn't really believe she will ever succeed. She has accepted the idea she will never amount to anything. She often speaks of herself in self-depreciating terms. She pours herself into her children, hoping they will value her.

The Price We Pay

Each of these relational patterns grows out of our focus on others and our subconscious attempts to control how they think of us. While these patterns are designed to get our needs met, they come with a huge price tag. Living out of *the fear of being hurt* isolates us from others as we live behind our walls, keeping others at an arm's length. We lose the joy of living in meaningful relationships. We lose ourselves when we live out of *the fear of being abandoned or rejected.* We sacrifice ourselves, surrendering our own thoughts, needs, and desires. In doing so, we give people power over us. Someone else determines our safeness, our value, and our happiness. Living out of the *fear of being inadequate, incapable, weak, and powerless* is exhausting. We create a façade that requires constant attention. It is also isolating as we do not allow anyone to get close enough to know our vulnerable self. Our love relationships suffer because we do not know how to be open and vulnerable. We miss the joy of deep friendships. We become slaves to other people's opinions when we live out of our *fear of being insignificant or less than.* We too give other people power over us. Constantly performing, achieving, and measuring up to expectations is also exhausting. It robs us of the freedom to live out of gifts and passions.

None of these patterns allow us to live freely out of our gifts and passions (i.e., our true selves). The greatest downside to all of these relational patterns is we never discover our true selves.

Discovering Your True Self involves recognizing our relational pattern and developing a healthier way of living. It teaches us to live with healthy boundaries, using our power to manage ourselves. Rather than focusing on and attempting to control others, the journey leads us to be self-responsible.

A Guide for Personal Reflection and Journaling, for Group Conversation and Discussion

- Review how power is used in relation to each of the four needs. For example, when our need is to be safe, we use our power to …
- What is your relational pattern? How do you use your power in relationship to others?

CHAPTER 9

RESIDUE FROM THE LAND OF THE GIANTS: EMOTIONALLY REACTIVE (WHEN FEAR TAKES OVER)

It was a good day. Alan had plans for dinner with friends, downtown, before going to a Cubs game at Wrigley Field. Tickets were purchased, plans made. Anticipation and excitement grew as the appointed time approached. And then it happened. A comment was made that literally took the air out of Alan's sails. Gone were the anticipation and excitement, replaced by a heavy feeling of depression and shame. Those heavy feelings hung over him throughout the evening, robbing him of any pleasure of being with his friends or any enjoyment of the game. The comment had pushed his button, triggering old feelings of depression and shame.

Each of us lives with a unique set of hot buttons in our emotional makeup. These hot buttons are places in which we are emotionally oversensitive. That sensitivity is the unhealed, unresolved pain of experiences from the land of the giants. They are tied to our dominant, driving fear. They trigger the anxiety with which we live. They are what set us off.

When our buttons are pushed, our high alert alarms go off. It is as though our greatest fear has become a reality. The old fear immediately becomes full blown, taking control of us. We overreact emotionally. Old emotional pain, accompanied by a torrent of old messages, is triggered in our psyche. Pain-laced fear, tied to old experiences and the emotional wounds they inflicted, explodes into the present like the eruption of a volcano. The past experience takes over the present moment, robbing the present of the gifts it has to offer. This reaction happens instantly and automatically without any conscious thought or decision. In such situations, the thinking part of the brain is completely bypassed. It is literally offline.

Alan's primary emotional need was to be valued. He was driven by the fear of being insignificant and unimportant. His hot button was anything that communicated he was flawed and no good. No one values a flawed, no-good nobody. The comment that was made pushed his hot button, triggering the old messages and old feelings. He descended into a spiral of shame. The pain of his past invaded his present situation, sabotaging it.

The term *hot button* suggests an overly emotional reaction. What would be a normal emotional reaction is exaggerated and dumped into the situation. The exaggerated emotional reaction takes over the situation. It overwhelms the individual and dominates his perspective.

Hitting our button can trigger the togetherness force. The reaction is excessive as togetherness is taken to excess.[25] We automatically turn to others, bonding together in a quest for comfort and assurance. Boundaries are blurred and individuality is surrendered as the different ones adapt to the larger group. Agreement and loyalty are expected. An adversarial *us-them* posture holds sway, accompanied by black-and-white, either/or thinking.

Similarly, hitting our button can trigger the individuality force. Again, the reaction is excessive as individuality is taken to the extreme. This reaction is expressed in withdrawing from others emotionally, even to the point of cutting oneself off from others emotionally or physically.[26] This reaction is an attempt to find a sense of safeness by avoiding the chaos of that particular relationship.

Hot buttons are often associated with anger. A volcanic explosion of anger, targeting the other, is one form of emotional reaction tied to our hot button, but it is not the only one. Our hot button can also trigger fear or shame or feelings of inadequacy or any combination of these. Chicken Little's "the sky is falling" is an example of fear being dumped on others as it dominated Chicken Little's perspective.[27] Alan's experience is an example of shame dominating his perspective and being dumped on his trip to the ball game.

The exaggerated emotional reaction may take an opposite direction. Rather than being out of control and dumping one's emotion onto the situation, the individual may simply shut down emotionally. Rather than outwardly expressing the emotion, the individual is seemingly disconnected from his emotions, not experiencing anything emotionally. The emotions are still very much alive, but they do not dominate the person or the situation. This shut-down reaction is often accompanied by taking charge or doing something to address the situation or by emotionally distancing from the situation.

Taking charge is a common reaction when the anxiety of our hot button is triggered. Taking charge is an attempt to control the situation as a way of reducing the anxiety it produces. It involves attempts to fix whatever is identified as wrong. Taking charge is often accompanied by finding fault with another person. The other is believed to be responsible for and is blamed for the situation. The blaming views the other as flawed or inadequate. Thus, the one taking charge overfunctions, doing what the other failed to do or did inadequately. The one who overfunctions gains a sense of being *better than* the other, who is treated as *less than* or no good.

Molly, Debra, Brad and Victor's normal relational pattern (Chapter 8) involves overfunctioning. When their hot buttons are pushed, they shift into overfunctioning overdrive. Bill and Vivian revert to emotional distance and cut off, while Mary dumps her anger on her husband with her nagging about his drinking.

Conflict: When Fear Invades a Relationship

Pushed buttons not only unleash emotional reactions, they often produce conflict. We often fail to recognize that underlying the conflict is our primary emotional need and its twin fear.

Disagreement is a normal, inescapable part of relationships. After all, we are all different. Those differences are often at odds with one another. Our primary emotional need determines how each of us approaches those differences. Those of us who live out of the need to belong tend to downplay the differences, often giving in to the other in order to avoid conflict.

Those of us who live out of the need for power or value (the individuality side of the togetherness—individuality continuum) tend to hold onto the differences as a way of "being me." We are almost always ready for a good fight. Learning to manage these differences in a mutually respectful way is one key to a healthy, enduring relationship.

When we fail to manage the differences, they escalate into conflict. Conflict is when the individuals involved take an adversarial stance toward one another over a particular difference. They each defend their position on the matter. The connection between them becomes strained. They temporarily sacrifice their togetherness in order to assert their individuality. On the togetherness—individuality continuum, they are living completely on the individuality side. The standoff continues until one becomes uncomfortable with the emotional distance and makes a move to get them back toward the togetherness side of the continuum

Conflict is a normal part of any relationship. More importantly, it is a necessary part of a growing relationship. Conflict provides an opportunity for the connection—the very thing being sacrificed in the conflict—to be strengthened and deepened. At the same time, the conflict raises the possibility of the relationship being damaged beyond repair.

> Conflict is a normal part of any relationship. More importantly, it is a necessary part of a growing relationship.

That damage occurs when the focus shifts from the differing positions to a focus on the other. That shift is expressed in "you" statements. "You always …" "You never …" Such statements are a form of attack against the other. They destroy the sense of safeness in the relationship by undermining the other's sense of value. At this point, the relationship is on dangerous ground.

Conflicts arise out of our differences, but something deeper is the real issue in the conflict. What we identify as the issue in the conflict is *not* the real issue. It is merely the surface issue—the topic or content over which we disagree. The real issue—the deeper, underlying issue—is our primary emotional need.

<u>Surface Issue: Topic of the Conflict</u>
Underlying Issue: Emotional Need

The conflict arises out of and is fueled by our dominant, driving fear. The old fear is triggered by the content of the conflict and how the other is responding to it. When we argue our position, what we really want is to have our primary need met so our dominant fear can be calmed. We want to be safe and not hurt. We want to be accepted and not abandoned. We want to feel capable and not inadequate. We want to be valued and not discounted.

As long as the conflict focuses on the surface issue (content), a battle of wills takes place. Each person takes an opposing position on the topic. For example, the argument is over spending (the content of the argument). One person wants a stricter oversight on the family budget; the other wants to buy what is needed, when it is needed or is on sale! The argument becomes about winning (i.e., convincing the other to embrace my position as "right"). Winning generally involves discounting the other's position. With both parties seeking to win, they both end up losing. They sacrifice the relationship while defending their position and attacking the other's. Resolution doesn't take place until one person surrenders their position in order to end the fighting and preserve the relationship. Generally, the one who surrenders does so in every conflict, regardless of the content of those conflicts.[28]

One way to get to genuine resolution and reconciliation is to talk about *interests* rather than arguing the merits of one's position.[29] While two people may take different sides on the surface issue (in this case spending), they may be able to identify interests they both can embrace. Regarding spending, one person's interest lies in not going into debt or depleting the savings. The means by which she seeks to protect this interest is in strict control of spending. The other's interest may be in meeting the family's needs. The means by which he seeks to address this interest is in spending whenever the opportunity arises, even if it means using a credit card to make the purchase. The conflict is over how to, the means by which they seek to ensure their interests are met. Talking about the underlying interests allows the two "adversaries" to find mutual ground. Hearing and respecting each other's interest allows the two to explore a means to getting those interests met beyond the positions they have taken and over which they have fought.

These interests reflect the deeper, underlying issue: each person's emotional need to be safe, to belong, to have power, to have value. Her desire for a strict control over spending is rooted in her need to be safe. But the way she seeks to meet that need—strict control of the spending—touches his need for power. Her desire for control robs him of any sense of power in making decisions, which stirs his sense of not being valued (trusted) in the relationship. His credit-based spending threatens her need to be safe. They are arguing positions rooted in their driving emotional need.

Genuine resolution and reconciliation are only possible when each person again feels safe, accepted, capable, or valued.

Learning to accept responsibility for myself and my part in any conflict is a part of our journey. It is also the path that deepens and strengthens the connection in the relationship as we learn to be vulnerable with one another. It helps us know one another more deeply. It helps us create safeness in the relationship as we honor the other's pain and fear.

A Guide for Personal Reflection and Journaling, for Group Conversation and Discussion

- Recall a time when your button got pushed. What was your reaction?
- What old messages are played when your button is pushed?
- Name your "buttons."
- What is the old fear associated with your buttons?
- Who is most adept at pushing your buttons?
- What is your normal pattern of reaction?
- Reflect on a recent experience of conflict. Identify your interest in the conflict.
- What is the deeper emotional issue to which that interest points?

CHAPTER 10
2 + 2 = 4

When we left the land of the giants, we carried with us the anxiety developed there along with the patterns we learned. The result was predictable. Just as 2 + 2 = 4, so anxiety plus old patterns results in a constructed self.

What is a constructed self?

The Constructed Self

What I call the constructed self is the persona we created out of our desire to be accepted and loved. This persona has been referred to as the pseudo self (Bowen) or the false self (Merton). Each of these terms suggests a persona that is not genuine or authentic. It is a self whose identity is tied to a group. The New Testament books of Ephesians and Colossians speak of the old self related to a previous way of life (Ephesians 4:21–23; Colossians 3:9–10). I view this old self as the constructed self. I use the term *constructed* because we manufactured this self based on others' directives.

Our constructed self is the only self many of us have ever known. Consequently, it is difficult for us to recognize it. It is simply who we are, except it is *not* who we really are. It is who the world trained us to be, not who God created us to be. It is who the world said we should be if we wanted to be accepted or loved. It is a public self we created to show to others. It is the persona that masquerades as who we are. It is a substitute for who we really are.

This constructed self stands in contrast to our true self, the self God created us to be. But most of us seldom know our true self because we are so tied to our constructed self.

> Our constructed self is who the world trained us to be, not who God created us to be.

Our awareness of this persona is reflected in the things we say. "If you really knew me, you wouldn't like me." "My filter wasn't in place when I said that." "I let my guard down." "I can't wait to get home and let my hair down."

We created this persona in response to the emotional pressures of the social world(s) in which we lived. Our first and primary social world was family. Beyond the family, we experienced emotional pressures from school, church, social groups, friends, and community. The emotional pressures we experienced in our family were generally duplicated and reinforced by the other social groups of our lives. At times, some of our groups held differing values and expectations. For example, one of the challenges of the early school years is learning and adapting to what is expected at school as opposed to what is acceptable at home.

Every social group, including family, lives with a set of expectations. These expectations are called by many names: values, family traditions, ethics, social codes, etiquette, standards, rules, guidelines, the party line, etc. If we were lucky, the expectations were clearly stated. Almost always, there were expectations beyond what were stated. These expectations defined what was expected of us as we lived within that particular relationship system.

Our various social groups used these expectations to judge us. How we were treated in the group was tied to how well we lived up to the expectations. Acceptance in the group was based upon how we conformed to the expectations. In other words, playing on the basic need to belong and the fear of rejection, acceptance was bartered in exchange for conformity. Standing or value in the group was tied to how well we measured up. The opposite was also true. Rejection was tied to the failure to conform. Frequently, the rejection was accompanied by some type of condemnation or shame. The condemnation played on our need to be valued along with our need to be viewed as capable. Rejection and condemnation by the group were the punishment the group doled out on us for our failure to conform.

The expectations of these social groups became the building materials we used to manufacture our constructed self. As we conformed to their expectations, we were constructing a public persona that was acceptable within that particular social group.[30] Anxiety drove our construction project. Our objective in creating this persona was to get our emotional needs met within that group. Wanting to belong, afraid of being left out, we conformed to the standards of these groups. We dared not challenge or violate their standards for fear of condemnation and rejection.

> The expectations of our social groups became the building materials we used to manufacture our constructed self.

We were acting out of our need to belong. We worked to achieve, based on their definitions of success. We were acting out of our need for a sense of power and ability. Our success, as they defined it, brought us respect and standing in the group. That respect spoke to our need to have value. As long as we played by the rules, we were relatively safe. We were acting out of our need to be safe. Not only did anxiety drive the manufacturing of our constructed self, it is also the fuel on which the constructed self runs.[31]

Some of us, frustrated with the social expectations of the group or culture, constructed a persona based on defiance and rebellion. We chose not to conform, enduring the condemnation and rejection of the group. Our constructed self was as the black sheep of the family or the rebel or the outlaw. We were often described as antisocial, defiant, uncooperative, stubborn, and hardheaded. Interestingly, in our rebellion, we generally found others who, like us, were rebels or rejects. Drawing from those with similar rebellious attitudes or outsider standings, we created our own group in which to belong.[32] We never escape our need to belong, even when our identity is the outsider.

A segment of society that has grown in size in the past half century is made up of youth and young adults who choose to live in rebellion against traditional accepted social norms. They adopt an alternative lifestyle that is reflected in their dress, hairstyle, tattoos, body piercings, music, and life choices. They have created an alternative culture that abandons the social mores that have been at the core of white, male-dominated American culture for generations. Interestingly, in their rebellion, their alternative lifestyle is still defined by those established cultural norms. Their lifestyle and choices proclaim, "We are not that!"

Society is made up of a wide variety of social groups, each based on different criteria. While the expectations of each vary, each one is grounded in our need to belong.

> Family, culture, society were the architects of the constructed self; we were the project managers putting it in place.

So our constructed self is who culture and society created us to be, based on what they said was important. Family, culture, and society were the architects of the constructed self; we were the project managers putting it in place.

But there are other dimensions to this constructed self.

The Ego-based Self

Our constructed self is an ego-based self.

The ego-based self is rooted in self-reliance, built through self-effort, tied to some external set of expectations, and based on merit. It deals in comparing and competing. Its goal is to "get it right" and to "be right." This approach to life engages and appeals to the ego, hence the term ego-based self.

This ego-based self is *merit based*. It lives out of a merit-based system focused on measuring up and failure, deals in rewards and punishments, and promotes performing, achieving, and producing. It operates out of *earning-deserving* thinking, both in evaluating self and relating to others. Earning-deserving thinking is *if … then* thinking. *If* we measure up to expectations, *then* we feel good about ourselves. *If* we fail, *then* we condemn ourselves. We reward or punish ourselves based on what we believe we deserve. Deserving, being a foundational concept in our thinking, is a frequent term in our speaking. "I don't deserve …" We also relate to others out of the same mentality. We give them what we think they deserve. These kinds of evaluation are evidence others' expectations have become internalized and are the basis of how we judge ourselves and others. They reflect the standard to which we seek to conform. These internalized expectations are expressed in the language of "need to," "ought to," "have to," "should," and "must." These "need to," "ought to" statements reflect what we understand it means to be "right."

Comparing and competing are inherent parts of merit-based thinking and, thus, inescapable parts of the constructed, ego-based self. We compare ourselves to others, focusing particularly on those who don't measure up to the standard(s) to which we conform. Those of us whose identity is tied to rebellion compare ourselves to those who conform to the standard we have rejected. This comparison produces a mentality of *us-them*. We associate with those like us, segregating ourselves from those who are different. Our constructed, ego-based self likes uniformity.

Comparing and competing involve evaluating. Which group is right? Which group is wrong? Whose way is best? Of course, the obvious answer (almost without fail) is we are right and the other is wrong. We are right. Our way is best. We often proclaim God to be on our side, quoting scripture to validate our position, thereby proving we are right.

Merit-based thinking, with its comparing, competing, and evaluating, leads to judging and condemning. The judging is tied to a *better than-less than* orientation. Because we are right and our way is best, we judge ourselves as *better than* the other, judging them as *less than* ourselves. Our evaluation fosters a not so subtle sense of superiority or arrogance to which we are generally blind. Our association with those like us, segregated from those who are different, reinforces our sense of being superior. Uniformity reinforces our sense of being right and *better than* those not like us.

Ultimately, merit-based thinking is about power and control. We attempt to control how others view and treat us, repeating the patterns we learned in the land of the giants. We broker conformity in exchange for their acceptance. And then we repeat the pattern with others, bartering acceptance in exchange for their conformity. We attempt to make them like us, reinforcing our sense of "being right" and *better than* those not like us.

For some of us, comparing and competing with its judging and condemning backfires. We judge ourselves as not measuring up to the expectations we have internalized. Failing to measure up, we condemn ourselves as flawed and no good. We punish ourselves with self-condemnation and self-hate. We live with a deep sense of shame and its debilitating companion, depression. Yet even such self-loathing is an expression of an ego-based self.

In summary, the constructed, ego-based self is merit based. It operates out of *earning-deserving, if … then* thinking. It deals in rewards and punishment. This merit orientation, with its *earning-deserving, if … then* thinking, translates into transactional relationships. Others are evaluated and judged, accepted or rejected, included or excluded based on how they conform to the expectations of the ego-based self. Living out of an *us-them* mentality, the ego-based self compares, competes, evaluates, judges, and condemns. It desires uniformity and sameness. A *better than-less than* orientation underlies how the constructed self views and relates to others. It survives on "doing it right" and "being right."

The carefully disguised spirit of the constructed, ego-based self is a self-serving, what's-in-it-for-me spirit.

The Shadow Self

The constructed, ego-based self always has a shadow side. The term *shadow* suggests this part of who we are is not as readily seen. It lurks in the shadows. We have to look intently to see it.

The shadow self is made up of those parts of self that are judged as unacceptable. It is composed of those places where we are weak, inadequate, and powerless. Our failures and how we don't measure up lurk in the shadow self. The shadow self includes the parts of our humanness that are judged as base, crass, uncouth, or unrefined. Simply put, the shadow self includes those parts of us that, when exposed, cause us embarrassment and shame.

Fear is the emotional tone of our shadow. It harbors our deepest fear: we are indeed unlovable, flawed, and no good. We are afraid we will be rejected and left out because of some imperfection and flaw. Being excluded proves we have no value. We are afraid and think, *If they really knew us, they would not love us.* We are afraid we have nothing of significance to offer, no real value on our own. We view our places of weakness and inadequacy as evidence these deep fears are true. No wonder we push these parts of ourselves outside our conscious awareness! Our shadow is permeated with the fear we will be found out!

The shadow self is the dwelling place of shame. Shame lurks in its darkness. Shame and guilt are often associated, but they are different. Guilt is about behavior; shame is about one's being. Guilt is a legitimate emotional experience related to a wrong act as defined by a social code or moral standard. It calls for self-reflection and change. Shame, in contrast, is wounding and paralyzing. Shame is the message we are indeed flawed, no good, and unlovable. It is the pain we feel when we think our deepest fear is true. Shame is the pain we feel about being human. (Shame was often used in our formative years when we failed to live up to the expectations of the giants, stirring anger in them. They used shame to motivate us to be better. Shame never works as a motivator. It only cripples. Merit-based cultures are generally shame-based cultures. Shame is the poison of merit-based thinking.)

Shame often manifests itself as depression. Depression is anger turned inward at oneself. It is a form of self-punishment. It robs us of peace and joy, condemning us to live under a cloud of debilitating negativity.

Shame makes our shadow a place of extreme sensitivity and pain. It contains the pain of old, unhealed wounds and the emotional memories of the events that caused them. It is the storage place of old messages that reinforce our shame. It is what stings when someone makes a condescending statement to us or about us. Our shadow is the place from which we react when our buttons are pushed. Our programmed emotional reactions are our effort to protect our ego from the pain and deep-seated shame with which we live.

I grew up in a large family in an agricultural community. My parents were part of the working class. My father dropped out of school in the eighth grade to help support his widowed mother and younger sister. He worked in construction, building and remodeling homes. Although he was a skilled craftsman, he jokingly referred to himself as "a wood butcher," denying his abilities. My mother was a high school graduate who worked in bookkeeping. She was a trusted "shade tree accountant" without the formal training or credentialing. They both were hard workers who sacrificed themselves to provide for their large family. Because of these and other factors, my parents did not enjoy the prestige of being a part of the socially elite of our community. They had no voice or standing. This heritage, along with being the second born son, was a factor in "value" being my primary emotional issue. Two old messages still live in the back of my mind; both say I am "no good." One was a critique of my work, calling it "shoddy work." The critique was coupled with the prediction "You'll never amount to anything if that's the kind of work you do." The other was by a high school coach who said to me, "You'll never be the football player your brother was" (one of the "gifts" of having an older sibling!). Any statement or action today that treats me as *less than* others or discounts what I have to offer pokes my shadow.

Dealing with Our Shadow

Because of the pain associated with our shadow, we find ways to avoid it.

We hide the undesirable parts of ourselves along with the shame we associate with them. We not only hide them from others, but we hide them from ourselves. These parts of ourselves make us uncomfortable. We don't like them. So we disown them, often pushing them out of our awareness. This subconscious denial is the way we protect ourselves from the pain associated with these unacceptable parts of our self. Pushing them out of our awareness, we don't have to face them or deal with their pain.

We seek to avoid our shadow side by judging and condemning others. Focusing on others' failures allows us to ignore our own. Their failures stand in contrast to the "right" and "good" we do. Judging and condemning others reinforces our sense of being *better than* them because we don't do the wrong they do. Judging others, viewing them as *less than* us, allows us to feel good about ourselves at the other's expense. After all, we are not *that!* We are not like them. We are better than that. This common means of avoiding our own shadow is reflected in Jesus's teaching about not seeing the log in our own eye while focusing on the speck in the other's eye (Matthew 7:1–5).[33]

Judging reflects the constructed, ego-based self's desire for sameness and uniformity. Associating with those who are "like me" while judging those who are different is another way we seek to avoid our shadow.

Avoiding the shadow explains the importance of status symbols. We use status symbols to offset the shame associated with our shadow. We tie our sense of value to a position or job, an achievement or recognition, socioeconomic status or wealth. Ironically, helping others we deem less fortunate can be a way of reinforcing that we are okay, allowing us to ignore our shadow. The very term *less fortunate* carries the sense of being *better than* them. It reflects a one-up position.

Some avoid the shadow by borrowing value from family and heritage. Others of us, especially when family is not a source of value, borrow value from the university we attended or from the church we attend or from the country club of which we are a member. The part of town in which we live, like our travel habits, can be status symbols that help us avoid our shadow.

Of course, avoiding the shadow is a foundational reason we constructed an ego-based self. Our constructed self ties our identity to a social group, allowing us to enjoy some of the value and power associated with the group. Belonging to the group allows us to feel okay about ourselves.

A popular way of avoiding the shadow is to hide it behind a religious veneer.

The Religious Self

Religious life is ripe with opportunities for manufacturing a constructed, ego-based self. All the aspects of the constructed, ego-based self can be found in a religious environment:

- standards of expectations
- the emphasis on conformity
- the merit orientation with its *earning-deserving, if ... then* thinking
- the *us-them* mentality that involves comparing and competing, judging and condemning
- the assumption we're right
- a *better than-less than* orientation.

Religious groups such as churches tend to focus on right belief, right behavior (morals), and right ritual. They emphasize external things that can be measured. They offer a clear standard to which to conform. This standard of what is "right" becomes a ready-made standard for comparing and competing, judging and condemning. The ego-based self latches onto these external measurements, finding in right belief, right behavior, and right ritual a safe place to hide the shadow self.

I do not mean to say every religious group functions out of a constructed self mentality (although some do). Most would proclaim beliefs that are the opposite of such a perspective: grace-based instead of merit-based, unconditional acceptance as opposed to *if… then* thinking, inclusive of all rather than *us-them*, nonjudgmental rather than *better than-less than*. But beliefs and practice do not always align.

The human ego is clever and deceptive. In spite of what a religious group teaches, the ego can hijack the context, constructing a religious identity that distinguishes itself from others (*us-them*) and judges itself to not be like "those people" (*better than-less than* orientation). It can use the church's beliefs and standards of moral behavior as a basis for judging others. In other words, the human ego can easily use religious life to manufacture a constructed, ego-based self with a religious veneer. The religious veneer is the ultimate trump card for being right and okay: the God factor. God's on my side![34]

Taking a Closer Look at the Constructed, Ego-Based Self

The constructed, ego-based self is the only self most of us have ever known. Consequently, most of us have never taken the time to examine it. It is simply who we are and the way things are in our life. But they are not the way things have to be! Consider these realities about the constructed, ego-based self.

The constructed, ego-based self is based on appearances and thus is a false self. It is not genuine or authentic. It is as authentic as many of us know how to be, but it still involves pretense. It focuses on externals while ignoring the internal dimensions of self. It spotlights strengths and ignores weakness.

Because it is based on appearances, the constructed, ego-based self is fragile. The constructed, ego-based self is too fragile to deal honestly with the shadow self. Anything that touches the shadow triggers intense emotional reactions designed to protect the ego.[35]

Because of its fragile nature, the constructed, ego-based self looks for others like it. It values sameness and uniformity. Diversity is a threat. It is easily threatened by those who are different and by those who hold different beliefs. It must be defended from anything that challenges the thinking upon which it is constructed. A challenge to any belief, especially religious belief, is a threat to being "right." Adamant beliefs and rigid positions are used to shore up its fragile nature. Attacking and demonizing those who hold opposing beliefs and positions are used to protect it.

The constructed, ego-based self is inherently resistant to new ways of thinking and, thereby, to learning, growth, and change. It is rigid and closed in its thinking.

The constructed, ego-based self is willing to sacrifice a relationship for the sake of "being right." This factor contributes to broken relationships on a personal level, to church splits on a social level, and to polarization on the denominational and national levels.

The constructed, ego-based self is dualistic in its thinking, seeing things from an either/or perspective. It operates out of a black and white, right or wrong, all or nothing perspective. This dualistic thinking is what makes diversity look like a threat. The constructed, ego-based self cannot see or tolerate any truth but its own.

For the constructed, ego-based self, competition is a way of life. Comparing and competing feeds its sense of being "right," okay, and *better than* others. It hates losing.

The constructed, ego-based self is more comfortable with doing than simply being. Thus, it values work and production over relationships. Unless it is being productive, it is wasting time. Even its recreation is doing oriented.

The constructed, ego-based self is an exhausting, draining way to live. It must be constantly maintained, reinforced, and defended. It is tied to externals. It is dependent on merit. It requires continuing conformity and achievement. It leads to a self-depleting pattern of "trying harder to do better." It underlies our addiction to being busy.

The constructed, ego-based self is isolating. It carries with it the fear of being truly known. Thus, it creates a lonely existence.

The constructed, ego-based self seeks validation through attention, acceptance, affection, approval, affirmation, and applause. Sometimes this effort to gain validation is sought through the accomplishments of our children and grandchildren.

The constructed, ego-based self produces a variety of negative feelings about self. It can create a "try harder, do better" mentality. We live with the awareness of falling short of some standard. Relying on self-effort, we resolve to try harder and do better. The resolve generally gives way to yet another failure that stirs yet more resolve. This pattern produces an endless cycle of trying harder and failing. This pattern can lead to settling. We give up any personal expectation of measuring up to the demands expressed in the behavior code. We settle for mediocrity, doing "as best I can." A sense of shame, accompanied by a spirit of self-loathing and self-punishment, often accompany these patterns. Perhaps the most dangerous result goes to the opposite extreme: spiritual blindness. The constructed, ego-based self is not aware of the subtle, "better than" arrogance with which it lives. This blindness is protected by a sense of self-satisfaction.

The constructed, ego-based self is allergic to healthy spirituality. Spiritual transformation involves recognizing and moving beyond this construction project and the ways of thinking that support it. So the constructed, ego-based self substitutes right belief, right behavior, and right ritual in place of spiritual growth. It focuses on externals that can be measured rather than the internal transformation that is the core component of spiritual growth. Consequently, it is an obstacle to spiritual maturity and a barrier to being able to love as Jesus loved.

At best, the constructed, ego-based self is a way of surviving. It is how we survived when we lived in the land of the giants. But it can never lead us beyond surviving into thriving. It cannot produce freedom or peace or joy. Emotional-relational-spiritual health requires us to move beyond these old survival mechanisms.

The constructed, ego-based self is often difficult to recognize in our own lives. The more successful we are in our world, whether economically, professionally, academically, or socially, the more difficult it is for us to see our constructed self. Some kind of pain or failure is often needed to help us honestly face the reality of the self we have manufactured.

The constructed, ego-based self blinds us to our true self, leaving our true self undiscovered.

The journey of *Discovering Your True Self* moves us beyond our constructed, ego-based self into the discovery of who God created us to be: our true self.

A Guide for Personal Reflection and Journaling, for Group Conversation and Discussion

<u>The Constructed Self</u>

- What were some of the social groups that shaped who you are?
- What brought their affirmation and applause? How was their disapproval expressed?

<u>The Constructed, Ego-Based Self</u>

- Listen for your use of the terms *need to, ought to, have to, should,* and *must.* Listen for your use of the word *deserve.* Become aware of how much these words are a part of your thinking.
- To what groups or individuals do you compare yourself?
- What groups or individuals do you judge, looking down on them as wrong? How are they failing to measure up to your expectations?

<u>The Shadow Self</u>

- What things live in your shadow?
- When do you encounter your shadow?
- Which of the identified methods do you use to avoid your shadow?
- What gives you a sense of pride?

<u>The Religious Self</u>

- Where have you seen the constructed, ego-based self in religious life?
- What other religious groups do you view as "them" or "wrong"?
- Why is it difficult to recognize our own constructed, ego-based self, particularly a religious version of it?

PART 2

THE JOURNEY

CHAPTER 11
LOOKING AT THE JOURNEY AHEAD

The journey of *Discovering Your True Self* leads us beyond the sabotaging, controlling power of anxiety and fear. It is a journey out of the constructed, ego-based self and all that contributed to its creation. It is a journey in which we experience transformation as we learn new ways of thinking and relating.

The goal of the journey is discovering and living out of the true self. Chapter 1 describes this goal. The chapters in this section describe the journey and what it entails. They speak of the emotional-relational-spiritual growth through which the true self is released. These chapters identify concepts, resources, and skills that make progress on the journey possible.

CHAPTER 12
FROM, INTO, BY MEANS OF

The journey of *Discovering Your True Self* is one of emotional-relational-spiritual growth. This growth process is commonly known as spiritual formation.

Every growth experience has three components. The first component is moving beyond what was. Growth moves us beyond the way(s) we lived before. We leave it behind, moving *from* what was. The second component is moving forward. Growth moves us beyond what was, forward *into* what is new and different. *Into* carries the idea of going through a doorway or entering a new realm. Growth ushers us into a new stage. A central factor in these two movements is learning. We move *from* what was *into* the new stage *by means of* learning, the acquiring of new knowledge and skills.

A young child, crawling around in the land of the giants, learns how to pull up and balance. That new skill allows him to begin to take steps, moving into the toddler stage while leaving behind the crawling stage. This three-dimensional pattern—*from, into, by means of*—is repeated throughout life as we move from one stage of life to another. Every time we move forward into something new, we leave behind what was. Learning lies at the heart of the process. Learning spawns the process and continues as we live into the new.

The author of the New Testament book of Ephesians identified these same three components as the essence of the spiritual transformation process. The author used the metaphor of changing clothes to describe the process.

> You were taught to put away your former way of life, *your old self,* corrupt and deluded by its lusts, and to be renewed in the spirit of your minds, and to clothe yourselves with *the new self,* created according to the likeness of God in true righteousness and holiness. (Ephesians 4:22–24; emphasis added)

Put away the old, clothe yourself with the new, by being renewed in the spirit of your minds: *from, into, by means of.*

Spiritual formation involves putting off the old self. The old self is described as a former way of living shaped (corrupted and deluded) by lusts. The word *lust* is generally associated with physical desires, particularly sexual desires. This understanding equates the old self with immoral behavior. Our constructed, ego-based self makes it difficult for most of us to identify with the concept of lusts. Lust and desire are a part of the shadow we seek to deny. Another way of thinking about lust is hungers. When the four basic needs are not met, they manifest themselves in the form of emotional hungers: the hunger for attention, acceptance, affection, achievement, appreciation, or applause. These emotional hungers, combined with the anxiety associated with the four basic needs, shape our constructed self.[36]

The first component of *Discovering Your True Self* is recognizing and putting off the self we manufactured out of our desire to be safe and belong, out of the desire for power and value. We deconstruct the constructed self. We leave behind the anxiety and the patterns we learned from living in the land of the giants. We move beyond *earning-deserving, if ... then* thinking, beyond merit-based relationships, beyond *us-them* mentality, beyond comparing and competing, judging and condemning, beyond having to be "right," beyond *better than-less than* orientation, beyond uniformity and sameness. We break free from shame and the old messages that reinforce it. We lay aside the veneer of the constructed, ego-based self. The journey moves us *from* an old way of thinking and living.

At the same time, the journey leads us *into* a new way of thinking, living, and relating. In the words of the biblical writer, we put on the new self. This new self is an emotionally-relationally-spiritually maturing self. It is who God is recreating us to be, fashioning us into the divine likeness. The new self is our true self.

Putting off and putting on is not a single act. It begins with a single act, a choice to begin the journey. The motivation behind our choice can be the pain associated with the old or the promise of what could be associated with the new. Generally, the motivation involves both the pain and the promise. But the choice must be made again and again. It must be made each time we are faced with moving *from* an old, familiar way so that we can move *into* a new, healthier way of being. In other words, putting off and putting on is an ongoing process that leads to transformation and maturity.

At the heart of this putting-off, putting-on pattern of transformation is learning. We move *from* the old *into* the new *by means of* learning new ways of thinking and living. We develop new understanding and new skills. The biblical writer placed this learning component between the statement about putting off the old self and putting on the new self: "to be renewed in the spirit of your minds" (Ephesians 4:23). The means by which such transformation takes places lies in learning a different way of thinking that leads to a different way of living and relating.

Moving beyond the old and into the new is only possible as we learn new, healthier ways of thinking and relating. We learn to live with healthy emotional boundaries. We learn to use our power to manage ourselves. We train ourselves to be self-aware and self-responsible. We find our sense of safeness within ourselves and in our relationship with God. We learn to live out of self-confidence and confident humility. We discover our gifts and passions, investing them to benefit others.

The outcome of this lifelong, spiritual process of transformation is emotional-relational-spiritual maturity that releases us to be who God created us (i.e., our true self).

A Guide for Personal Reflection and Journaling, for Group Conversation and Discussion

- Reflect on a growth experience, identifying *from* what you moved *into* what you moved.
- What learning fueled that experience?
- How are you different because of the experience?
- What do you do to pursue new learning to fuel additional growth?

CHAPTER 13

THE RENEWING OF THE MIND: TURNING LOOSE OF STINKING THINKING

At the heart of the transformation process is learning to think differently. We move *from* the old *into* the new *by means of* learning new ways of thinking that lead to new ways of living. Rather than reacting out of anxiety and fear, we begin to choose healthier, more appropriate, and more productive responses.

In his letter to the churches in Rome, the apostle Paul wrote of the importance of learning to think differently. "Do not be conformed to this world, but be transformed *by the renewing of your minds*" (Romans 12:2; emphasis added). The original Greek translated as "do not be conformed" carries the idea of "stop being conformed." The conforming had already taken place. The world had already shaped their thinking. Paul urged his readers to move beyond how their world had trained them to think and live. They were to be transformed as a caterpillar is transformed into a butterfly.[37] The catalyst of that transformation was the renewing of the mind.

The world, through our experience in the land of the giants, has shaped how we think and, consequently, how we live. Our thinking was overwhelmed by anxiety, the old fear we would again be hurt by being left out or abandoned, by being inadequate and not measuring up, by not being valued and treated as *less than*. We learned to live out of merit-reward, *if . . . then* thinking that deals in rewards and punishment. Merit-based thinking naturally produced transactional relationships. Thinking in terms of *us-them* and *better than-less than*, we developed a competitive mind-set. We were trained to think in terms of scarcity (there's not enough for everyone to have a share) rather than abundance. Thus, we were driven to make sure we got our share. All the while, we lived with the deep fear our shadow side would be known, revealing how we didn't measure up and were, consequently, undeserving and *less than*. This kind of anxiety-driven thinking is what undergirds the constructed, ego-based self and sabotages our relationships. Anxiety-driven thinking is stinking thinking.

The religious term *repentance* captures the idea of the renewing of the mind. Repentance is generally associated with behavior, but the Greek term translated as repentance (*metanoia*) speaks of thinking, not behavior. The Greek carries the idea of thinking with a different mind. Behavior cannot change significantly until the underlying thinking changes. Thinking differently leads to acting differently.

The Hebrew term for repentance (*shub*) carries the idea of turning back or returning. In repentance, we turn *from* the way we are currently living by turning back *to* God. We turn from our anxiety-shaped, merit-based ways of thinking and living to embrace God's ways of grace. We move *from* the merit-based thinking and living of the constructed, ego-based self *into* the true self *by means of* the renewing of the mind: learning to think from a God-shaped, not fear-based, perspective.

The journey of *Discovering Your True Self* calls us to move beyond our old way of thinking (stinking thinking) to discover and embrace a different way of thinking that leads to emotional-relational-spiritual growth, to healthy relationships, and to the releasing of the true self.

A Guide for Personal Reflection and Journaling, for Group Conversation and Discussion

- Identify one way in which you have moved beyond how you were taught to think or what you were taught to believe.
- What led you to that different way of thinking?
- Identify a way of thinking or a belief that challenges or threatens what you believe.
- Identify a way of thinking or a belief to which you tightly hold and you passionately defend.

CHAPTER 14
TURNING LOOSE OF STINKING THINKING ABOUT SELF

Stinking thinking is an appropriate term for the way we have been trained to think. It leads to hiding the true self beneath the veneer of a constructed, ego-based self. It produces bondage, not freedom; death, not life. Such thinking certainly stinks.

Stinking thinking is the lens through which most of us see ourselves. Seeing ourselves through the eyes of the giants, most of us were trained to think of ourselves negatively. The child who lives with ADD learns to think of himself as flawed because he can't sit still as adults in many settings demand. The young teenage girl lives with body shame because she sees herself as fat, a product of the unrealistic Barbie Mattel culture. The child who struggles to learn the way other children learn sees himself as stupid (i.e., flawed and inadequate). The child who is born second views himself as having less value than the firstborn. The younger child believes herself to be inadequate as she attempts to keep up with her sister who is five years older. Being inadequate translates into being flawed, which morphs into being no good and unlovable. The older sister, displaced by a new baby who gets all the attention, learns to tie her value to being a good big sister who takes care of the younger sibling. The child who feels overlooked grows up thinking she is has no value. The child who is constantly corrected thinks of himself as flawed and incapable of doing anything right. The child who enjoys the applause of his parents for his accomplishments gets the subtle message he only has value when he achieves and measures up to their expectations. He learns to hate his failures and hide his struggles. The blessed child enjoys the attention and privilege but carries the burden of having to excel and achieve. The princess basks in being the center of attention but fears those situations in which she is not. Deep within, she does not know who she really is.

Each of these negative messages, and many more like them, tell us we are not acceptable or lovable *just as we are.* Something must be changed or corrected if we are to be accepted and belong. As a result, we hide who were really are (i.e., our actual thoughts, feelings, and desires) behind the mask of conformity. We use our power to gain acceptance and belonging, a sense of value and significance by complying with the expectations placed on us in the land of the giants. We construct a pretend self that reflects what the giants say we should be if we want to be a "good" boy or girl who is recognized and praised. In this process, we lose our true self.

These negative messages are lies, but as children, we had no way of knowing it. We had nothing to challenge the lie or instruct us differently. As a result, these lies became a part of our construction project (i.e., the persona we created in order to be safe and to belong). And they continue to haunt our psyche even though we are adults. Inside our adult bodies lives an emotionally wounded child who still falls prey to the lies. These lies are what keep the constructed, ego-based self in place. They fuel the anxiety with which we live.

Progress on the journey of *Discovering Your True Self* is made as we recognize and reject the lies, embracing a healthier, truth-based perspective to displace them. Offsetting the lies we believe is the teaching of scripture about who we are.

- We were created by God. "For it was you who formed my inward parts; you knit me together in my mother's womb. I praise you, for I am fearfully and wonderfully made. Wonderful are your works; that I know very well. My frame was not hidden from you, when I was being made in secret, intricately woven in the depths of the earth. Your eyes beheld my unformed substance" (Psalm 139:13–16).
- We were created by God, in the image of God. "So God created humankind in his image, in the image of God he created them;

male and female he created them" (Genesis 1:27). "In the image of God" suggests we were created for relationship with God. A divine spark was planted within each of us so that we might participate in and share God's life of love.

- Because we are God's creation, we along with all of creation are innately "good," not sinful or evil. "God saw everything that he had made, and indeed, it was very good" (Genesis 1:31).[38]

- We have been claimed by God in Christ Jesus as God's beloved children. "See what love the Father has given us, that we should be called children of God; and that is what we are. Beloved, we are God's children now" (1 John 3:1–2).[39]

- We have been called to be the followers of Jesus, learning and living the ways of God Jesus taught and lived (the ways of the kingdom).[40]

- The Spirit of God dwells in us. "And I will ask the Father, and he will give you another Advocate, to be with you forever. This is the Spirit of truth, whom the world cannot receive, because it neither sees him nor knows him. You know him, because he abides with you, and he will be in you" (John 14:16–17).[41]

- God's Spirit is at work in us, recreating us into the likeness of Jesus. "And all of us … are being transformed into the same image from one degree of glory to another; for this comes from the Lord, the Spirit" (2 Corinthians 3:18). "Beloved, we are God's children now; what we will be has not yet been revealed. What we do know is this: when he is revealed, we will be like him, for we will see him as he is" (1 John 3:2).[42]

- God's Spirit has given each of us special gifts and abilities to use in ministry to others. "To each is given the manifestation of the Spirit for the common good. All these are activated by one and the same Spirit, who allots to each one individually just as the Spirit chooses" (1 Corinthians 12:7, 11).[43]

- God's Spirit empowers us to live the ways of God, using our gifts to make a difference in the life of another in Jesus's name. "You will receive power when the Holy Spirit has come upon you" (Acts 1:8).

- As the children of God and the followers of Jesus, equipped with the Spirit's gifts and power, we are God's partners in the world, doing God's work in the world. "Very truly, I tell you, the one who believes in me will also do the works that I do and, in fact, will do greater works than these" (John 14:12).

Making progress in *Discovering Your True Self* occurs as we embrace and live out of who the scripture (God) says we are, refusing to give power to the lies. But the lies have deep roots in our psyche. They are not easily uprooted. The constructed, ego-based self does not die quietly. It is the self, albeit a pseudo self, we manufactured in order to belong and have value. Our sense of place is tied to it as is our sense of standing and value. Our success and accomplishments are evidence of our capability and power. To move beyond the constructed, ego-based self requires the discovery of a new, more reliable source for our safeness and belonging, our power and worth. It leads us to live by faith in a different, God-oriented reality as opposed to the false certainty tied to following the rules.

Moving beyond the constructed, ego-based self is a spiritual endeavor. It is what releases the true self. It is an inescapable part of being a follower of Jesus and of the spiritual journey. Jesus taught,

> If any want to become my followers, let them deny themselves and take up their cross and follow me. For those who want to save their life will lose it, and those who lose their life for my sake will find it. For what will it profit them if they gain the whole world but forfeit their life? (Matthew 16:24–26)

Understanding the concept of the constructed, ego-based self guides our understanding of this teaching. Inserting the language of constructed self and true self in his statement brings clarity.

> If any want to become my followers, let them deny the self they have constructed based on the world's values and

social pressures, take up their cross, and follow me. For
those who want to protect the standing in the world's eyes
of their constructed, ego-based self will lose their true self,
and those who surrender their constructed, ego-based self
for my sake will find their true self. For what will it profit
them to gain the world's power, standing, fame, prestige,
wealth, approval, or applause yet forfeit their true self?

To deny self is to surrender the status and standing one has gained
in the eyes of others as the basis of one's identity. It is to pursue a new
identity tied to Jesus and his teachings. To deny self and to take up the
cross express the same idea. The cross was an instrument of death reserved
for insurrectionists against Rome. To take up the cross was and is to
renounce the merit-based ways of the world. It is to live out of step with
the shame-based culture in which we live. To follow Jesus was and is to
learn from him a different way of living, based on the ways of God known
as the kingdom of God.

Moving beyond the constructed, ego-based self does not mean we
discount or disregard what we have accomplished in the world or our place
in the world. Rather, it means we no longer tie our sense of value and worth
to them. They no longer are the basis of our identity, our sense of self.
Our sense of who we are is tied to something more enduring and eternal:
we are a beloved child of God, called to live as the follower of Jesus and
as God's partner in the world, equipped and empowered by God's Spirit
who lives within us.

Moving beyond the constructed, ego-based self is only possible as we
abandon merit-based thinking and living. Discovering our authentic, true
self takes place as we learn to live out of grace.

A Guide for Personal Reflection and Journaling, for Group Conversation and Discussion

- What are some of the factors that shaped your sense of identity?
- What are some of the old, negative messages about yourself that you carry?

- Review the ten dimensions of a God-based identity. Which statement is most difficult for you to embrace?
- What makes it difficult to embrace and live out of this God-shaped identity?
- What practice can you adopt to foster this God-shaped identity within you?

CHAPTER 15
TURNING LOOSE OF STINKING THINKING ABOUT MERIT-BASED LIVING

Merit-based thinking and living is the foundation of the constructed, ego-based self. We manufactured our false self by following the practices of merit-based thinking and living. The lies we believed and the negative perceptions of self they created are the products of merit-based thinking.

Merit-based thinking, as we have seen, is essentially about measuring up. It focuses on achieving and accomplishing, producing and performing. At the core of this way of thinking is some standard of expectation by which we are judged. Conformity is what is expected, yea, demanded. Merit-based thinking deals in rewards and punishment. It speaks the language of deserving. What we receive, whether good or bad, is what we deserve, based on how well we measured up. Merit-based thinking relies totally on self-effort. Consequently, it appeals to the ego.

The Process Nature of Life

A fundamental flaw in merit-based thinking is it goes against what it means to be human. We humans, like all living things, were created with the capacity to grow and develop. We do not come into the world fully grown. Trees and plants begin as seeds. They grow by stages into maturity, at which time they bear fruit. Animals and fowl begin as babies, growing through various stages into maturity. Like all living things, we begin as infants and grow through various stages of development into maturity.

The merit-based lies dictating our lives neglect this process nature of life, replacing it with expectations and demands. Often, the expectations by which we are judged exceed our stage of development. I think of how often a child is expected to act like an adult, sitting quietly and reverently (?) in a worship service using adult language and adult images. How often do adults (the giants) assume a child knows better and reprimands them for doing something no one has taught them to do? How often are adult expectations of children based on what makes life easier for the adult rather than what is appropriate for a child? And how often are we critical of ourselves for not measuring up without giving ourselves the opportunity to learn and grow into the expectation? The merit-based thinking that undergirds the constructed, ego-based self emphasizes measuring up and conforming to expectations. The very nature of life calls for nurturing, guiding, and teaching through the multiple stages of development that lead to maturity.

Progress in *Discovering Your True Self* occurs as we embrace our humanness with its inherent limitations and process nature. Embracing our humanness requires us to set aside merit-based thinking for a different way of thinking. That different way of thinking is found in learning the ways of God Jesus taught.

The Grace-Based Ways of God

The ways of God stand in contrast to the anxiety-producing, anxiety-driven, merit-based ways inherent to our human condition. In an ancient oracle, an unidentified Hebrew prophet described that contrast.

> For my thoughts are not your thoughts,
> nor are your ways my ways, says the LORD.
> For as the heavens are higher than the earth,
> so are my ways higher than your ways
> and my thoughts than your thoughts. (Isaiah 55:8–9)

We make progress as we learn the ways of God, allowing them to shape our thinking and, thereby, how we live in relationships.

The ways of God are an expression of the character of God.[44] Everything God does is governed by God's divine character. The Hebrew scriptures describe God's character as compassionate and gracious (Exodus 34:6). The Christian scriptures describe God's character as love (1 John 4:7–8). Those of us who are followers of Jesus believe God's character is most fully revealed in Jesus of Nazareth.[45] Jesus revealed God to be a servant kind of God, a God who uses power to serve.[46]

Grace is foundational to the ways of God. It speaks of how God lives in relationship with us. It is God's relational pattern. Grace stands in stark contrast to merit-based thinking. Grace speaks of a love that is unconditional and undeserved. God loves us because it is God's nature to love, not because of what we have done or not done. Such love stands in stark contrast to the concept of deserving. Grace speaks of gift. All of creation is a gift of God's love, given freely, to be received with joy and gratitude.[47] Gift stands in stark contrast to the concept of earning. Grace speaks of generosity and abundance. Generosity stands in stark contrast to the merit-based, measured doling out of what one deserves. Abundance stands in stark contrast to the scarcity thinking inherit to self-effort and self-reliance. Grace speaks of unfailing faithfulness.[48] God will never give up on us or abandon us. Faithfulness stands in stark contrast to the fragile nature of acceptance bartered in exchange for conformity.

Grace is expressed in forgiveness. God forgives freely and lavishly. Forgiveness is the way God deals with the failures that are a normal part of any growth process, including what is commonly called sin and rebellion! In forgiving, God refuses to allow the failure to be a barrier in the relationship with us. Forgiveness stands in stark contrast to the judging, condemning, shaming, and punishing that grow out of merit-based thinking.

Grace and forgiveness point to God's unswerving commitment to nurture our growth and development. God's promise is to bring us to full maturity, a maturity that mirrors God's own nature of self-giving, servant love.[49] Thus, God's concern is not on how well we measure up but on what we are learning and how we are growing. God's forgiveness allows our experience of failure and sin to become a learning experience through which we grow. As we grow emotionally-relationally-spiritually, we will measure up. Through the Spirit's redeeming, transforming work, we will become like Jesus, possessing God's nature as our own, freeing us to love as Jesus loved.

Grace can also be used in reference to how God uses God's power (i.e., God's sovereignty). Because how God uses power is always governed by God's character of self-giving, servant love, God always uses power to create life and to nurture that life into maturity and wholeness. In our lives, God works to grow us up emotionally-relationally-spiritually. God works in and through every experience, particularly the

> God's sovereignty is expressed in using whatever happens to help us grow emotionally-relationally-spiritually.

challenging, painful experiences, to transform them into occasions for progress and growth.[50] Nothing lies outside of God's power to redeem for our good. God's sovereignty over all things is expressed not in determining what happens but in using whatever happens to help us grow emotionally-relationally-spiitually.

Living out of these realities is freeing. Grace and forgiveness provide us a way to move beyond the sabotaging power of anxiety. They set us free from the pressure to perform and achieve. Grace empowers us to deal differently with the experience of failure along with the guilt and shame the failure generates. We no longer have to be crippled by their power. Grace sets us free to deal realistically with our shadow without the fear and shame that are tied to it. It allows the shadow to become an arena for insight and growth. Grace sets us free from the pressure associated with self-effort. Grace sets us free from the need to compare and compete. Grace sets us free to experiment, explore, and risk. Most importantly, grace sets us free to learn and grow.[51]

A Guide for Personal Reflection and Journaling, for Group Conversation and Discussion

- Our culture operates on merit-based thinking. Give some examples.
- Where do you recognize merit-based thinking in your own life?

- How much is the process nature of life a part of your thinking? How does it manifest itself?
- How do you define God's grace?
- Relate how you have experienced God's grace in your life.
- What stirs in you when you think of God's unwavering commitment to your growth and development, leading you into a Christlike maturity?
- What is your understanding of the sovereignty of God? How does the author's description of God's sovereignty contribute to your understanding? What implications does the sovereignty of God have for your journey?
- Contrast the results of merit-based thinking to grace-based thinking.

CHAPTER 16
TURNING LOOSE OF STINKING THINKING ABOUT US-THEM, BETTER THAN-LESS THAN

Merit-based thinking produces *us-them* thinking and its corresponding ways of relating: comparing and competing, judging and evaluating (*better than-less than* thinking), accepting and rejecting. We move beyond these old ways of relating (*from*) as we learn to live out of our new identity (*by means of*): we are the beloved children of God, claimed by God's grace in Christ Jesus, equipped and empowered by God's Spirit. Our relationships take on a new pattern (*into*) as we learn to live out of grace and forgiveness.

In place of *us-them* thinking, we learn to view and embrace others as being like us: God's creation and God's beloved child.[52] We no longer make relationships dependent on sameness as this deeper sameness governs the way we view the other. Differences are no longer viewed as a threat to be feared. We no longer have to retreat into the false security of uniformity, segregating ourselves from those who are not like us. Rather, diversity is viewed as a normal part of God's creation and embraced as a pathway to greater understanding and wholeness. We explore the differences with curiosity and respect in an effort to know and be known. We accept struggle and misunderstanding as a normal part of living in relationship. Living out of grace and forgiveness, we refuse to give up on the other or abandon the relationship. Viewing the other as a developing, in-process, not yet mature human being (just as we are), we move beyond the judging, criticizing, and condemning that are inherent to our human condition and part of our merit-based thinking. We learn to be patience and understanding, gentle and kind, generous and faithful in the relationship.[53] In short, we seek to live as a more emotionally-relationally-spiritually mature human being. We seek to love as Jesus loved.

Obviously, we have to learn to live into this way of thinking and relating. It is a process, a journey. Struggle and failure will be a part of our effort because merit-based thinking is deeply ingrained in our psyche. Rather than seeing the struggle and failure through the lens of merit-based thinking, we view them from the perspective of God's grace and forgiveness. The struggle and failure invite us to turn to the Spirit for insight into ourselves that will lead to further growth. We turn to the Spirit for the power to do what we cannot do in our own strength. Thus, the struggle and failure become an opportunity for growth.

A Guide for Personal Reflection and Journaling, for Group Conversation and Discussion

- Identify someone or some group you view as "other" and have difficulty embracing.
- What makes it difficult for you to embrace the "other"?
- What would it take to see and relate to the "other" as a beloved child of God? What would it take to live in relationship with them?

CHAPTER 17

TURNING LOOSE OF STINKING THINKING ABOUT UNIFORMITY AND SAMENESS AS THE PATH TO BEING SAFE

A natural product of merit-based thinking is associating with those like us. We are attracted to those who think like we think and value what we value. We prefer uniformity over diversity, sameness over differences.

This preference for uniformity plays a strategic role in the constructed, ego-based self. It is how we attempt to meet our need to be safe. Our association with others like us reinforces our sense of being "right" and okay. It quiets our anxiety about being flawed and no good. It allows us to avoid the challenge of those who are different from us. In doing so, it provides us a false, fragile sense of being safe and secure.

The fragile nature of our security is revealed in our reactions to those who are different, particularly to those who hold different views and opinions. We perceive such people as a threat. Their different opinions carry the implied threat our position is wrong. This implication is a threat to our constructed, ego-based self that prizes being "right." If our position is wrong, then we are flawed. Our constructed, ego-based self begins to crumble.[54]

The fragile nature of this uniformity-based security is the product of flawed thinking. "If I am right, then you must be wrong." This kind of thinking is dualistic thinking. It is either/or thinking. Truth must be one or the other; it cannot be both. But truth is always greater than my understanding of it, greater than the other's understanding of it. There is always more to truth than what we know. There is always more to learn, if we are willing to learn and grow!

Dualistic thinking blocks our ability to learn from those who are different. New insights and deeper understanding are gifts that come with diversity. In contrast, our association with those like us simply reinforces and solidifies our position. It seldom challenges us or leads us into new insights. The renewing of the mind leads us beyond dualistic, either/or thinking so that we can learn from all of life's diversity. It leads us out of the fragile, false security provided through uniformity.

The constructed, ego-based self does not know real safeness. In the absence of real safeness, it seeks certainty and stability. Both reflect our desire to be in control. Certainty is about being "right" (i.e., beliefs). Stability is found in predictable sameness, such as routines and traditions. Certainty and stability are protected by being rigid in one's beliefs, practices, and habits. Unsurprisingly, any kind of change is a threat. As diversity is a threat to the security we seek through sameness, so change is a threat to the security we seek through certainty and stability.

Meeting the Need to Be Safe without Being in Control

Uniformity and sameness, certainty and stability grow out of our need to be in control. They are ways we seek to meet our need to be safe. The need to be safe, as we saw in Part 1, is one of our four basic emotional needs, if not our primary need. As we make progress on the journey and the true self begins to emerge, we move beyond our futile attempts to be in control so that we can feel safe. We learn a healthier way to meet this need.

The safeness of the true self is not dependent on others. It finds its sense of being safe in two sources.

The first source lies in changing how we use our personal power. Rather than seeking to control others or the situation (i.e., be in control), we learn to use our power to manage ourselves. We use our power to set healthy boundaries and be self-responsible. Learning to manage ourselves allows us to live with inner peace. Such peace can be experienced even in the midst of anxiety-producing experiences. Healthy boundaries and being self-responsible are keys to authentic relationships and genuine safeness within them. We will explore these concepts in the next two chapters. Chapter 20 addresses living with inner peace. Accessing inner peace is a key component to living out of a sense of being safe. Inner peace is tied to the second source, faith.

The second source of safeness for the true self is faith. Faith is the settled belief, deep trust, and quiet confidence in God's faithfulness. Faith finds reassurance in God's promises. It is expressed by living in harmony with God's truth that contradicts the conventional wisdom of the world. Faith is confirmed as we experience God's faithfulness in the midst of life's challenges.

Faith rests in God's promise to be with us. This promise is a recurring theme in Hebrew and Christian traditions. The Hebrew name Emmanuel means "God with us." The psalmist proclaimed the unshakeable, inescapable presence of God.

> Where can I go from your spirit?
> Or where can I flee from your presence?
> If I ascend to heaven, you are there;
> if I make my bed in Sheol (the realm of the dead), you
> are there.
> If I take the wings of the morning
> and settle at the farthest limits of the sea,
> even there your hand shall lead me,
> and your right hand shall hold me fast.
> If I say, 'Surely the darkness shall cover me,
> and the light around me become night',
> even the darkness is not dark to you;
> the night is as bright as the day,
> for darkness is as light to you. (Psalm 139:7–11)

In the Farewell Discourses of John, Jesus promised, "I will not leave you orphaned" (John 14:18). He spoke of abiding in us (John 14:23) through the Spirit who dwells in us (John 14:16–17). The New Testament book of Matthew records Jesus promise, "I will be with you always, even to the end of the world" (Matthew 28:20). God is with us and will never abandon us.

God's presence sustains us in the midst of life's challenges, providing us strength for the challenge. The prophet Isaiah spoke of such strength to a people who felt abandoned and forgotten by God.

> Why do you say, O Jacob, and speak, O Israel, "My way is hidden from the LORD, and my right is disregarded by my God"? Have you not known? Have you not heard? The LORD is the everlasting God, the Creator of the ends of the earth. He does not faint or grow weary; his understanding is unsearchable. He gives power to the faint, and strengthens the powerless. Even youths will faint and be weary, and the young will fall exhausted; but those who wait for the LORD shall renew their strength, they shall mount up with wings like eagles, they shall run and not be weary, they shall walk and not faint. (Isaiah 40:27–31)

The promised strength empowers us to rise above the challenge (mount up on wings like eagles) or to make progress in it without being depleted (run and not be weary) or to simply put one foot in front of another without being overwhelmed (walk and not faint). God's presence strengthens us on the journey. God's presence also gives us peace in the midst of the challenge.[55]

Faith rests in God's sovereignty and unswerving commitment to helping us grow emotionally-relationally-spiritually, as described above. God promises to work in and through every situation, redeeming and transforming even the most painful of experiences into a means of spiritual progress and blessing.[56] God's sovereignty is exercised not in protecting us from life's challenges and pain but in redeeming and transforming what those challenges do to us. Because nothing is outside of God's ability to transform and redeem, nothing is wasted.

Faith rests in God's extravagant generosity and the abundance of the kingdom. These twin realities lie behind Jesus's exhortation to not worry about the material aspects of life in Matthew 7:25–33 and Luke 12:22–34.

The stories of the feeding of the 5,000 and the 4,000 (Mark 6:34–45 and 8:1–9) proclaim the abundance found in the kingdom.

These two realities stand in stark contrast to the scarcity thinking that is a natural part of the constructed, ego-based self. The constructed, ego-based self relies upon self-effort and thinks from the perspective of deserving. Both scream, "Not enough!" There is a limit to what self-reliance and self-effort can produce. In a highly competitive world, there is a limit to what one can gain through producing, achieving, and performing (deserving). The fear of "not enough" spawns an insatiable desire for more.[57] Scarcity thinking seeks a sense of safeness in accumulating material wealth, something Jesus constantly challenged.[58] No amount of wealth provides the deep inner peace of being safe.

The true self anchors its sense of safeness in God: faith in God, in God's faithful presence, in God's sovereignty, and in God's generosity. As the true self emerges, we move beyond the physical, material dimensions of life as our primary focus. We are committed to emotional-relational-spiritual development that leads to healthy relationships. We seek to make a meaningful difference in the lives of others. We move beyond worry, freeing us to give with God's kind of generosity. We move beyond calculated, stingy giving into joyous generosity. We trust God's abundant provision, knowing that, in the kingdom economy, giving and sharing are a means of multiplication, not a form of subtraction that diminishes.[59] Trust in God's generosity and abundance stands in contrast to the fear-driven scarcity thinking of the constructed, ego-based self.

The need to be safe is foundational. As we make progress on the journey of *Discovering Your True Self,* we learn to meet this need through faith in God's faithfulness coupled with a Spirit-empowered ability to be self-responsible and set healthy boundaries.

A Guide for Personal Reflection and Journaling, for Group Conversation and Discussion

- This chapter speaks to our fundamental need to be safe. What makes you feel safe?
- How are certainty and stability expressed in your life?

- What do you experience when you do not feel safe? What do you do in those times?
- What is your reaction to the author tying our desire for safeness to our preference to uniformity and sameness?
- Review what the author said about faith as a source of safeness. "Faith rests in …" Identify examples of the link between faith and safeness from your own experience.

CHAPTER 18
GOOD FENCES MAKE GOOD NEIGHBORS: LIVING WITH HEALTHY BOUNDARIES

In ranching country, good fences are important. Good fences keep each neighbor's livestock on their own land. When fences are down, my livestock end up grazing on my neighbor's land. In other words, my neighbor feeds my livestock, without getting paid for it! While such an arrangement is good for me, my neighbor is not particularly happy about it. He generally complains, "Your cattle are in my pasture!"

Good fences are important in relationships too. Fences represent *ownership*, what is mine and what is yours. They represent *responsibility*, that for which I am responsible and for which you are responsible. They represent the scope of *power*, those things over which I have power and control and those things over which I don't.

Fences in relationships are called *emotional boundaries*. Emotional boundaries identify where you begin and I end. They define the limits of my ownership, responsibility, and power. In every dimension of life, ownership, responsibility, and power go together. If it is mine, I alone am responsible for it and I alone have power over it.

Three questions clarify an emotional boundary: Whose is it? Who is responsible for it? Who has power or control over it? When healthy boundaries are in place, the answer to these three questions will all be the same. "It is mine. I am responsible for it. I alone have power over it." If the answers to these three questions are different, boundaries are blurred; the fences are down. No clear distinction exists between the two persos.

91

Healthy relationships require healthy boundaries. Without clear, healthy boundaries, I assume responsibility for what belongs to you and attempt to control

> Whose is it?
> Who is responsible for it? Who has power or control over it?

what is yours—as you do with what is mine. Who is responsible for what and who has control over what becomes muddled and confused. Our fences are down. The relationship is unhealthy.

When the Fences Are Down: Living with Unhealthy Boundaries

Living in the land of the giants trained us to live with unhealthy boundaries. It trained us to believe we were responsible for the giants' happiness or anger. (We weren't.) It trained us to believe we had power over and, thereby, could control what they felt and did. (We can't.) As a result, the constructed, ego-based self does not understand or live with healthy boundaries. Boundary violations are a way of life for the constructed, ego-based self.

Boundary violations take two primary forms: dumping and robbing. Both are common in relationships. *Dumping* means I make you responsible for what is mine. I dump what is mine on you. (Remember ownership, responsibility, and power go together.) "You make me so angry" is an example of dumping. The anger is mine, but I make you responsible for it. The toddler throwing a temper tantrum dumps his anger on his parents in an attempt to get them to do what he wants. In judging others, we dump our expectations on the other. *Robbing* is the opposite of dumping. Robbing means I assume responsibility for what is yours. Parents commonly assume responsibility for what belongs to their children. "Have you done your homework?" "Did you get your jacket?" Diana (chapter 8) assumes responsibility for her husband's drinking. Through her nagging, she attempts to have control over it.

Sometimes, we follow both patterns in a single interchange. In "you need to" and "you ought to" statements, we dump our expectations on the other while assuming responsibility for and attempting to control what they do (robbing).

In boundary violations, responsibility and power are inseparable. When I make another person responsible for my anger, I give them the power to make me angry or happy. When I assume responsibility for what belongs to another, I attempt to control the other. They now have the power to please me or anger me.

Robbing is a basic pattern for the person who overfunctions. The overfunctioner assumes responsibility for something that is not his. Dumping is the basic pattern for the one who underfunctions. The underfunctioner abdicates responsibility for what is his. Both dumping and robbing are attempts to control the other. Until we learn to live with healthy boundaries, we all practice both patterns.

The lack of healthy boundaries pulls relationships to the togetherness side of the togetherness—individuality seesaw. We become fused with the other, sensitive to and reacting to every move. Their emotional reactions automatically trigger a predictable reaction in us as our reactions do in them. We are tethered together by an emotional cord so that any movement by one impacts the other. It is as though we are bound together in an emotional chain gang. A baby mobile illustrates how this principle works in a group. When something touches one figure of the mobile, all of the other figures are affected. They begin to jiggle too. Similarly, the lack of emotional boundaries in relationships causes us to "jiggle" whenever something stirs anxiety in the other. We are emotionally tied together. We are emotionally fused.

Not understanding the principle of boundaries, we seek alternate ways to create space (individuality) in the relationship. These alternate ways are attempts to manage the anxiety created by too much togetherness. The most common way is emotional distance. We emotionally withdraw from the other, staying emotionally aloof and isolated. We are not emotionally present to the other. Emotional distance is often paired with physical distance. We are simply not there. We avoid the strain (i.e., the anxiety and tension) in the relationship through work or busyness or the children's activities or hobbies or sports or exercise. Silence, humor, and drinking are often used as substitutes for boundaries.

Every problem in a relationship, any stress in a relationship involves a violation of boundaries. In every conflict and every battle of the wills, boundaries are being violated. The fences are down; your cattle are in my pasture.

Healthy boundaries are an essential aspect in the seesaw balancing act between the togetherness force and the individuality force (chapter 4). Healthy boundaries are what make healthy individuality possible. Healthy individuality makes healthy togetherness possible. Healthy boundaries are an essential dimension of healthy relationships.

Learning to live with healthy (or healthier) boundaries is a foundational principle and an indispensable part of the journey of *Discovering Your True Self.* Learning about healthy boundaries is *the means by* which we move *from* relationships filled with anxiety, frustration, and stress *into* healthy, meaningful relationships.

Healthy boundaries open the door to being self-responsible.

A Guide for Personal Reflection and Journaling, for Group Conversation and Discussion

- Relate your understanding of boundaries. From where did you gain your understanding?
- Identify an example of how someone dumped and robbed in their relationship with you.
- Which pattern are you most likely to practice: dumping or robbing? Give examples of how you do so.
- What fuels that pattern?

CHAPTER 19
SELF-RESPONSIBLE

Ownership, responsibility, and power belong together. Consequently, one of the outcomes of living with healthy boundaries is being self-responsible. We use our *power* to be *responsible* for that which is *ours*. We own responsibility for our thoughts and opinions, our perceptions, our feelings, our desires, our reactions, our decisions, and our actions.

In learning to be self-responsible, we move beyond the pattern we learned in the land of the giants. We let go of being responsible *for* the other. We abandon our attempts to control what the other thinks or feels about us along with our attempts to control what they do.

As we move *into* being more self-responsible, we move *from* the patterns that are a part of unhealthy boundaries: dumping and robbing.

We move away from dumping onto others, making them responsible for what is rightfully ours. A common way of dumping on others is judging them. In judging, we dump our expectations on them. Judging is generally expressed in "you" statements that accuse and blame the other. "You" statements are also used when we are dumping our fear, our opinions, and our desires on others. "You" statements appear to focus on the other, but in reality, they are attempts to protect our constructed, ego-based self. They attack the other and communicate we are "right" and they are "wrong." "You" statements attempt to bend the other to our will. They are attempts to control the other. Being self-responsible leads us beyond attempting to bring the other in line with our desires and expectations.

Being self-responsible also means we resist the urge to rob the other of what is rightfully theirs. We refuse to take responsibility for what belongs to them. We stop telling, instructing, commanding, and advising them on what they should do and how to do it. "You should ..." "You ought to ..." "You need to ..." Being responsible for what belongs to the other is an attempt to control them.

Another part of being self-responsible is being responsible *to* the other. Instead of being responsible *for* what the other thinks, feels, or does, we learn to be responsible *to* the other. Being responsible to the other means we communicate what we think and what we want. We learn to use "I" statements that clearly state where we stand. "I think ..." "I feel ..." "I want ..." "I choose ..." At the same time, we learn to respect the other person's thoughts, opinions, feelings, desires, and decisions. Clear "I" statements, coupled with respect for the other person's thoughts and opinions, place us in a position to negotiate a relationship in which the emotional needs of both are honored and met. In being responsible *to* the other, we do our part to keep the relationship healthy and vibrant.

This way of being responsible *to* the other person also helps us stay in a difficult relationship rather than abandoning it. It helps us negotiate the challenges that are a normal part of relationships. As appropriate, we apologize, owning responsibility for our inappropriate statements and harmful actions. We own responsibility for our feelings without blaming the other for them. We forgive, refusing to hold the other responsible for our hurt or give them power over our sense of safeness or happiness. In working through relationship challenges, we deepen the trust that is foundational to the relationship.

Using healthy boundaries to be self-responsible also helps us deal others' attempts to dump their issues on us or rob us of what is rightfully ours. We no longer allow others to control us and direct us. We learn not to personalize their criticisms and judgments, allowing them to affect or wound us (i.e., touch our old issues). Understanding boundaries empowers us to see their criticisms and judgments as efforts to control us. We understand their criticisms say more about *them* than about us.

For some of us, being self-responsible means learning *to have* thoughts, opinions, and desires. Many of us learned to surrender what we think, feel, and want in our effort to take care of the other and keep them happy. This pattern has become so deeply ingrained we are no longer aware of our own thoughts, opinions, or desires. For us, becoming self-responsible means becoming a self that reclaims what we have surrendered in our effort to be accepted and belong, in our effort to be safe.

But in order to be self-responsible, we must be self-aware.

Self-Awareness

Self-awareness is awareness of the interior dimension of our lives. It is the awareness of what we are experiencing emotionally in the midst of a situation, as it is happening. It is recognizing the fear and anxiety, the frustration and anger that have been triggered within us.[60]

Initially, self-awareness is about recognizing the emotional reaction we are experiencing in a particular situation. That recognition provides the opportunity to manage the reaction rather than automatically repeating it.

Self-awareness also involves recognizing the thinking that is behind our automatic reaction. Every emotional reaction is fueled by how we perceive the situation. Our perception or interpretation of the event touches old memories of similar experiences from our past. That memory, in turn, triggers the anxiety associated with those old memories. We subconsciously tell ourselves "it's happening again," thereby launching our emotional reaction.

perception → old memory → triggered anxiety → emotional reaction

All of this—the perception, the memory, the triggered anxiety, and emotional reaction—happens in an instant. It happens automatically and subconsciously, bypassing our conscious thinking. In other words, it happens outside of our awareness.

Self-awareness means we train ourselves to be aware of that which is initially outside our awareness. We learn to be aware of what we are experiencing internally, as we are experiencing it. We become conscious of what is happening subconsciously. This ability is a skill we cultivate and develop through practice. In other words, self-awareness is always trained self-awareness.

Self-Understanding

Trained self-awareness is built upon self-understanding. The more we know ourselves, the greater will be our ability to live with self-awareness. Self-understanding involves knowing our primary emotional need and its corresponding fear. It involves knowing our relational pattern (i.e., how we use our power in relationships to get our primary need met). It involves knowing our triggers and how we react emotionally when those triggers are tripped. In short, self-understanding is being aware of our ego-based, constructed self. The more we know ourselves, the more we are able to recognize when the old ways kick in. Self-understanding positions us to live with trained self-awareness.

self-understanding → self-awareness

Self-Management

Self-awareness creates an opportunity ripe with possibility for progress and growth. It presents us with a choice: in the midst of a situation in which old reactive patterns have been triggered, will we continue the old reactive pattern *or* choose a different, healthier response guided by principle? Self-awareness becomes the platform for changing how we have been conditioned to react. But such change requires us to manage our old reactions and the anxiety fueling them. It requires us to move beyond these old, automatic reactions so that we can consciously choose how we will respond. Self-awareness invites us to practice self-management.

Self-management is consciously choosing to not give power to the anxiety that has been triggered. It is recognizing the anxiety that is raging inside but choosing not to vent it or act on it. It is also about managing how we have learned to react when our anxiety is triggered. It is monitoring what we say and do so that it is not an expression of the triggered anxiety. Self-management moves beyond the automatic reactions, driven by anxiety, to consciously choose a healthier response.

The practice of self-management requires a shift from automatic reactions (like my fear response to the rattlesnake) to clearer thinking in which conscious choices can be made. A simple tool to use in making this shift is controlled deep breathing. Awareness of the anxiety (self-awareness) becomes a call to regain control of ourselves through controlled deep breathing. We breathe deeply through our noses, using our diaphragm to slowly inhale. With lungs full of oxygen, we hold our breath for three to ten seconds. Then again using our diaphragm, we slowly release our breath through our mouths. We repeat this process three times or until the anxiety subsides. This process puts us in control of something that is generally automatic and subconscious (i.e., our breathing). It also resets the brain, shifting from the automatic reactionary mode to the conscious, thinking mode. It reroutes the blood flow in the brain from the reactive centers to the thinking center.

Practicing self-management allows us to be self-responsible.

self-understanding → self-awareness → self-management = self-responsible

Self-Differentiation

Self-differentiation is a central concept in Bowen Family System theory. While it has become known outside of Bowen circles, it is often used in ways contrary to its original meaning in BFST.

In Bowen theory, self-differentiation is something one practices *in the midst of* a highly anxious situation. It is a consciously chosen way of responding and relating. It is an expression of self-management. Self-differentiation is *not* a status a person achieves. "I am a self-differentiated person." Such statements indicate the person does not understand self-differentiation. Self-differentiation is something one does, not a trait one possesses.

Self-differentiation is an effort, in the midst of an anxious situation, to be a separate self, operating out of clear, principle-based thinking. It is the effort to resist the togetherness forces that suck us into the fusion of boundary-less relationships. To do so requires us to not get caught up in the anxiety and the automatic, anxiety-driven reactions that take over anxious situations. Self-differentiation requires us to manage our own automatic reactions when our anxiety is triggered. It moves beyond the reactive behaviors anxiety produces: anger, polarization, defensiveness, "you" statements, attacks, blaming, shut down, etc. Self-differentiation is the effort to create a healthy individuality, using healthy boundaries, so that a healthy, unfused togetherness can be achieved. It is the pursuit of a healthy relationship when the relationship is disrupted and has become troubled.

Authentic self-differentiation has three dimensions to it. Self-differentiation is, in a highly anxious relationship or situation, the ability

- to function out of a principle-shaped "I" position
- while staying connected and in relationship with the other
- and maintaining the "I" position and connection until the anxiety subsides and the issues are resolved (persistence).[61]

Authentic self-differentiation requires us to practice self-management. It is a way of being self-responsible in a relationship.

self-awareness → self-management → self-differentiation = self-responsible

Self-Confidence

Living in the land of the giants trained us to focus our attention on others and to use our power to control them. Emotional-relational-spiritual development reverses these patterns. Rather than focusing on others, we learn to live with self-awareness. Rather than attempting to control what others think, feel, or do, we learn to use our power to manage ourselves. We manage our anxiety, our anxious thinking, and our anxiety-driven emotional reactions. We learn to make healthy choices, using healthy boundaries as a guide. Exercising self-awareness and self-management enable us to be self-responsible. The combination of self-awareness, self-management, and being self-responsible produces self-confidence.

Self-confidence is what the term implies: confidence in myself and in my abilities. Self-confidence is a quiet, inner strength that grows out of the knowledge that I can use my abilities to address my own emotional needs. I am not incapable or powerless. I am not a helpless victim of circumstances.

I can act on my own behalf. Self-confidence includes permission to use my abilities on my own behalf without being selfish or self-centered.

This inner strength is the opposite of the powerlessness and frustration we experience whenever we attempt to control others. The effort to control what others think, feel, or do is an exercise in futility that leaves us frustrated. It creates a battle of wills or emasculates the will of the other. It keeps us stuck in unhealthy relational patterns we learned in the land of the giants. In other words, attempting to control others is an indicator of unhealthy boundaries and emotionally immature functioning. It undermines the possibility of a healthy relationship.

Self-confidence is sometimes viewed as arrogance, but the two are not the same. Arrogance is the spirit of being *better than* or superior to others. It reflects a competitive spirit that finds its sense of value in comparing itself to others. It masks a deep fear of being flawed and no good, incapable and *less than*. Self-confidence has nothing to do with comparisons to others. It is independent of who others are or what they can do. Self-confidence is simply about oneself and one's own abilities to manage one's self in a healthy, responsible way.

Healthy self-confidence is a trait of the true self. As such, it is a product of emotional-relational-spiritual growth and an indication of becoming more emotionally-relationally-spiritually healthy. It grows out of one's relationship with God.

Self-confidence and being self-responsible go hand and hand with faith. Self-confidence includes awareness of what we *cannot* do as well as what we can do. Knowing what we cannot do in our own strength, we willingly turn to God for strength beyond our own. We open ourselves to the Spirit's transforming, empowering work within us. We know we cannot practice self-awareness or self-management apart from the Spirit's power and direction. Thus, we live out of a spirit of glad dependency on God. Our self-confidence grows out of our confidence in God.

self-awareness + self-management = self-responsible → self-confident

A Guide for Personal Reflection and Journaling, for Group Conversation and Discussion

Self-Responsible

- Describe the relationship between healthy boundaries and being self-responsible.
- What is the difference between being responsible *to* someone and *for* someone? Give an example of both from your own experience.
- Be aware of your use of "you" statements. What agenda is reflected in a "you" statement?

Self-Awareness

- Self-awareness is foundational to changing our behavior. Why is this so? Share an example from your own experience.
- Self-awareness is always trained self-awareness. What do you do to train yourself to be more self-aware?

Self-Understanding

- Explain the relationship between self-awareness and self-understanding.
- Identify aspects about yourself that you know: primary emotional need, driving fear, reactionary pattern, relational pattern, how you manage your anxiety (anxiety binders), pattern of boundary violations, etc.
- What experiences and training have contributed to your sense of self-understanding?

Self-Management

- Relate an experience of practicing self-management.
- What practices help you exercise self-management?

Self-Differentiation

- What is self-differentiation?
- Explain the relationship between self-management and self-differentiation.
- Relate an experience of exercising self-differentiation.

Self-Confidence

- What is the meaning of being self-confident?
- What is the difference between self-confidence and arrogance?
- What has contributed to your sense of self-confidence or lack of it?

CHAPTER 20
LIVING OUT OF THE PEACE OF CHRIST

Self-management, a key component to being self-responsible, is the means by which we move beyond anxiety into peace. Peace meets our need to be safe.

In the self-management section of Chapter 19, the concept of controlled deep breathing was presented as a tool that can disrupt the flow of anxiety in our brain. Controlled deep breathing helps to reset the brain from its reactive mode to its thinking mode. Experiencing peace in the midst of an anxious situation is possible through deep breathing and one additional step: breath prayer.

Breath prayer is using the controlled deep breathing as a guide to prayer. As we inhale, we pray, "Fill me." As we exhale, we pray, "Cleanse me." With each controlled deep breath, we pray (following the fruit of the Spirit as a guide), "Fill me with your love; cleanse me of my reactivity. Fill me with your joy; cleanse me of my frustration and anger and negativity. Fill me with your peace; cleanse me of my anxiety and fear." This kind of breath prayer helps us to become centered again. It helps us refocus on God and God's faithfulness, the true source of our safeness. We place ourselves in a position to experience peace—God's peace. We experience peace in the midst of the very situation that triggered our anxiety-driven emotional reaction.

Jesus promised us such peace. "Peace I leave with you; my peace I give to you. I do not give to you as the world gives. Do not let your hearts be troubled, and do not let them be afraid" (John 14:27). The apostle Paul also spoke of such peace.

> Do not worry about anything, but in everything by prayer
> and supplication with thanksgiving let your requests be
> made known to God. And the peace of God, which
> surpasses all understanding, will guard your hearts and
> your minds in Christ Jesus. (Philippians 4:6–7)

Paul identified the experience of God's peace as the result of prayer with thanksgiving. Thanksgiving calls us to look over our shoulder at the past. It leads us to remember our experience of God's faithfulness in previous experiences. Thus, prayer with thanksgiving helps us shift our focus from the anxiety-filled situation back to God, the source of our peace, and to God's faithfulness, the foundation of our peace.

In both of the texts about peace, the experience of peace is set opposite the experience of anxiety. Jesus spoke of anxiety as troubled, fearful hearts; Paul spoke of it as worry. We cannot experience anxiety and peace at the same time. One must give way to the other. Both texts called the readers to move beyond anxiety: "do not." The original language carries the idea of "Stop! Your hearts are troubled and afraid. You are worrying. Stop!" Anxiety is a normal dimension of life. We cannot avoid it. But being aware of it, we can refuse to live out of it. We can choose to move beyond its power through the exercise of self-management. We can pray, using breath prayer to disrupt the flow of anxiety and place ourselves in a position to experience God's peace.

What Jesus called "my peace" and Paul called "the peace of God" is an inner quietness that takes the place of anxiety's nebulous feeling of dis-ease. It displaces the fear, stilling the inner turmoil and settling the inner restlessness. Thus, the peace of Christ sets us free from the power of anxiety and fear, breaking their control over us. It sets us free from fear-based thinking and fear-based reactivity. It frees us to think clearly so that we can choose what we will do and how we will respond.

Exercising self-management so that we can experience God's peace in the midst of an anxious situation is a huge step on the journey. The more we practice it, the more natural it becomes. But peace in the midst of an anxious situation is not the ultimate goal. The experience of peace positions us to be a peacemaker.

Blessed Are the Peacemakers

Our breath prayer moves us into a position to experience God's peace. It puts us in a position for the Spirit to produce God's peace in us. Our prayer also invites the Spirit to work in us and through us in the midst of the situation. The Spirit produces God's peace in us *so that ...!*

Peace positions us to respond differently in the situation. To say the same thing with different words: self-management positions us to practice self-differentiation. Moving beyond the power of anxiety, we no longer contribute our reactivity to the chaos of the anxiety-filled interaction. We do not react to the others' reactivity. We are in a position to respond in a way that reduces the anxiety of the situation, calms the chaos, leads to clarity and understanding, and makes resolution possible.[62] Peace positions us to be a catalyst for healing, progress, and growth.

The Spirit produces God's peace in us so that we can be peacemakers in the world!

Cultivating the Peace of Christ

Breath prayer puts us in a position for the Spirit to produce the peace of Christ within us in the midst of an anxious situation. Breath prayer is a shorthand expression of meditation.

Meditation is a wordless form of prayer that seeks to move beyond the busyness of the mind. In meditation, we set aside the mind's work of planning and evaluating. We turn loose of being in control. Our only agenda is to be present to God as we rest in God's presence. Meditation incorporates intentional stillness and quietness so that we can be attentive to the moment and to what is inside us. We seek to be present to ourselves and to the moment as the pathway to being present to God. In our meditation, we seek to simply be rather than do.

Meditation is counter to the performance, achievement-orientation of the constructed, ego-based self. Consequently, attempting to practice meditation can be frustrating initially. The mind (the ego) likes to jump into the silence, reasserting its control. It disrupts the stillness with its racing thoughts. These common experiences can lead us to believe we are failing in our efforts to meditate. These thoughts are expressions of our performance, achievement-oriented thinking. They are the ego's way of accusing us we are not doing it right. And they can lead us to give up. Meditation is not about achieving some state of mind. Rather, it is an expression of our desire to live in relationship with God. It expresses our intent to attune ourselves to God and the Spirit's work. Thus, our recognition that the mind (ego) has reasserted itself is evidence that we are being self-aware. It becomes an invitation to practice self-management by centering ourselves again in God's presence.

Meditation is a vital tool in the transformation process. The anxiety-based thinking that produced the constructed, ego-based self is our default setting. It automatically "boots up" within us. In meditation, we offset this automatic default. Our meditation becomes a virus protector that isolates and quarantines our anxiety-based thinking with its lies. In meditation, we center ourselves in God and in the grace of God. We ground ourselves anew in God's grace and in God's truth, displacing the lies fueling our shame-filled shadow. We reclaim our identity in Christ as a beloved child of God, called to be a follower of Jesus, equipped and empowered with God's Spirit to live as God's partner in bringing the kingdom into reality. We learn to rest in God. We learn to trust God. We attune ourselves to God and renew our focus on living the ways of God.

Such resting in God nurtures our openness to the Spirit. It prepares us to live out of peace as we go about our routines and responsibilities. Centering ourselves through the regular practice of meditation trains us to access peace when anxiety stirs within us. Because our practice of meditation has trained us to rest in God's peace, breath prayer becomes an effective shorthand means of accessing the Spirit's peace throughout the day.

The peace of Christ allows us to move beyond the constructed, ego-based self and the anxiety that sustains it. It allows the true self to emerge and blossom.

A Guide for Personal Reflection and Journaling, for Group Conversation and Discussion

- Relate an experience in which you have experienced the peace of Christ in the midst of an anxiety-filled situation.
- How did your experience of peace help you in the situation?

- What is the relationship between experiencing the peace of Christ and being a peacemaker?
- What do you do to cultivate the peace of Christ in your life?
- Practice using breath prayer to rest in God's love and experience the peace of Christ.

CHAPTER 21
THE HEART OF THE MATTER

At the heart of our journey of *Discovering Your True Self* is an inner transformation, the transformation of the heart. This transformation is reflected in the spirit out of which we live.

The constructed, ego-based self is preoccupied with behavior: measuring up, conforming, achieving, performing, and doing it right. It focuses on the external realm that can be measured and graded. Our journey beyond the constructed, ego-based self leads us into the interior realm where we deal with the attitudes and spirit out of which we live. The interior realm, the heart, is what governs how we live. It is the core of who we are deep inside. It is the domain of the ego.

Jesus identified the heart as the source of evil behavior. "It is from within, from the human heart, that evil intentions come: fornication, theft, murder, adultery, avarice, wickedness, deceit, licentiousness, envy, slander, pride, folly. All these things come from within, and they defile a person" (Mark 7:21–23). In another teaching, he spoke of how a tree's nature determined its fruit (Matthew 7:16–20). His teaching instructs us to look beyond behavior to one's basic nature (i.e., what is in the heart).

Our journey of *Discovering Your True Self* moves us beyond a focus on external behavior to deal with the interior realm of attitudes and spirit. It leads us toward the transformation of what is in the heart and the spirit out of which we live.

The spirit of the constructed, ego-based self is fueled by anxiety. Every aspect of the constructed, ego-based self is designed to protect us from being exposed and hurt again. Our spirit is a self-protective spirit. As such, it is self-focused and self-serving. The intent of the constructed, ego-based self is to get our primary need met through others. Thus, our spirit is a self-centered, what's-in-it-for-me spirit.

Because the heart is the realm of the ego, what is in the heart reflects the ego's self-focused, self-serving, self-centered, what's-in-it-for-me nature. This self-focused, self-serving, self-centered, what's-in-it-for-me spirit is so deeply embedded we cannot escape it. It colors everything we do, even those things we do to help others. It often infects and perverts our religious involvement. Our journey of *Discovering Your True Self* leads us toward the transformation of this innate, what's-in-it-for-me spirit.

The spirit of the true self stands in contrast to the what's-in-it-for-me spirit of the constructed, ego-based self. The spirit of the true self reflects its spiritual nature. It is a Christlike spirit that is expressed in self-giving, servant love. Grace and forgiveness, along with compassion and kindness, flow freely from it. It is full of joy and peace. Gratitude and thanksgiving, in response to God's abundant grace and generosity, color it.

The New Testament letter of Colossians speaks of this spirit as a product of spiritual formation. The writer used the image of changing clothes (as in Ephesians 4) to describe spiritual transformation: having "stripped off the old self with its practices and have clothed yourselves with the new self, which is being renewed in knowledge according to the image of its creator" (Colossians 3:9–10). The new self, which I identify as the true self, is clothed with the Spirit of Christ. The writer identified the clothing with which we are to dress.

> As God's chosen ones, holy and beloved, clothe yourselves with compassion, kindness, humility, meekness, and patience. Bear with one another and, if anyone has a complaint against another, forgive each other; just as the Lord has forgiven you, so you also must forgive. Above all, clothe yourselves with love, which binds everything together in perfect harmony. And let the peace of Christ rule in your hearts, to which indeed you were called in the one body. And be thankful. (Colossians 3:12–15)

The Christlike spirit of the true self, grounded in its spiritual nature, is not the result of self-effort (the foundational piece of the constructed, ego-based self). No amount of self-effort can produce such a spirit. Self-effort—the exercise of the will—is only effective in changing behavior. It cannot change what is in the heart. Only the Spirit can change the heart.

Thus, our journey is a spiritual journey. The transformation it produces is only possible as we live in intentional relationship with God, opening our hearts and minds to the transforming work of the Spirit. We cannot transform our own hearts or the spirit out of which we live, but we can place ourselves in a position for the Spirit to do so.

Central to the Spirit's transforming work, as we have already seen, is the renewing of the mind. Learning the ways of

> Self-effort cannot change what is in the heart. Only the Spirit can change the heart.

God Jesus taught opens us to the Spirit's work. Learning the truths does not produce growth in and of itself. The growth comes as we struggle with how the truths challenge our thinking and beliefs and as we struggle to live out of them. Acknowledging our struggle to God gives the Spirit permission to work in us, moving us *from, into.* Acknowledging our struggle is like signing a permission slip before surgery, giving the doctor permission to do the surgery. Through the Spirit's work, the spiritual truth and principles begin to be internalized. These internalized truths empower us, as we practice Spirit-guided self-awareness and self-management, to move beyond our automatic, anxiety-driven emotional reactions and choose a healthier response. They guide how we choose to respond. We begin to live differently, guided by truths the Spirit taught us.

The Christlike spirit grows out of the truth the Spirit teaches us. It reflects the character of God as well as the teaching and ministry of Jesus. It is expressed in compassion, grace, and forgiveness. It guides us to use power to serve, making a difference in the lives of others. (In the Hebrew scriptures, the term for the servant use of power is *justice*.) It invariably calls us to use power on behalf of the powerless, particularly the poor and dispossessed within society. It leads us to love as Jesus loved.

Discovering Your True Self leads us to possess and live out of the spirit of Christ. It leads to a transformed heart.

A Guide for Personal Reflection and Journaling, for Group Conversation and Discussion

- What do you do to cultivate awareness of the interior realm of the heart?
- When have you been aware of the self-focused, self-serving nature of the constructed self in your own experience?
- Identify an area in which you struggle to live out of the teachings of Jesus. Share your struggle with God in prayer.
- Reflect and meditate on Colossians 3:9–15. Note which phrase(s) hold meaning for you.

PART 3

LIVING OUT OF THE TRUE SELF

CHAPTER 22
EXPERIENCING LIFE DIFFERENTLY

The true self is the person God created us to be. It encompasses our gifts and abilities, our interests and passions, along with our unique personalities. The true self emerges as we make progress on the journey. It is set free as the Spirit transforms our heart, ingraining Christ's nature in the core of our being. The result of the Spirit's work is a beautiful creation: the grandeur of God's character expressed through the uniqueness of our individual personality. We are set free to use our gifts in an area of passion to express God's love in the world. We live as God's partners in God's redemptive enterprise.

We have seen the transformation of the heart and the emergence of the true self free us to love as Jesus loved. Compassion, grace, and forgiveness become central to our lives, shaping how we view and treat others. We use the many aspects of our power to make a difference in the life of another as we live out of a spirit of joyous generosity. But there is more!

As we make progress on the journey, not only is the heart transformed but so is our experience of life. Spiritual truths train us to live out of a perspective untainted by the sabotaging power of anxiety. We see and respond to the experiences of life differently. A fuller, richer life opens up to us. Living more and more out of the true self, we

- embrace our humanness, both its strengths and its weaknesses
- enjoy deeper, more meaningful relationships
- experience joy, peace, and thanksgiving as the dominant emotional tone of our lives

- embrace pain and suffering, seeking to receive the gifts they hold as we depend on God for the strength, wisdom, guidance, and peace to deal with them
- move beyond the fear of death.

The renewing of the mind and the transformation of the heart lead us to experience life differently. The next chapters explore how life becomes different as the true self emerges.

A Guide for Personal Reflection and Journaling, for Group Conversation and Discussion

- How are you different because of your spiritual journey?
- How do you experience life differently because of your spiritual journey?

CHAPTER 23
BEING HUMAN

As we make progress on our journey, we learn to see ourselves through the eyes of God rather than through the eyes of the giants.[63] We learn to not give power to the lies expressed in old messages about being inadequate, no good, and unlovable. Those lies are countered with spiritual truth and a less skewed view of reality. The impact on how we live is significant. We learn to embrace our humanness, laying aside shame and self-hate. We learn to live with confident humility as we recognize and embrace our gifts and passions. We find meaning and purpose as we use our gifts and abilities to make a difference in the life of another in Jesus's name.

Embracing Our Humanness

Most of us, on some level, are uncomfortable with being human. One of the earliest stories in Hebrew scripture describes the desire to escape our humanness, using the false promise. "You shall be like God" (i.e., no longer human) (Genesis 3:5).

Being human appears to be a mixed bag. On one hand, we as humans have an intellectual capability not found in other creatures. We have the capacity for imagination and creativity. We can accomplish almost anything we can conceptualize, including probing the dark recesses of outer space. We have indeed been created in the image of God (Genesis 1:26). But being human also includes limitations, weaknesses, and needs. We are often powerless or feel we are. We are still very much "in process," not yet fully grown. Parts of us are still immature and undeveloped. And on top of these aspects of our humanness, most of us are emotionally wounded. These aspects of our humanness give birth to our anxiety and fear. They translate into struggle and failure. In relationships, they frequently produce conflict, broken relationships, and division. No wonder we fear these aspects of our humanness! No wonder we consider ourselves to be broken!

Being human is especially distasteful to the constructed, ego-based self. The weaknesses, limitations, and needs are viewed as evidence our deepest fears are true: we are inadequate, no good, and unlovable. It seems inevitable that we will be hurt. We have seen how the constructed, ego-based self hides these aspects of our humanness in the shadow self while presenting a persona that is appealing and respectable. It lives with a sense of shame about limitations, weaknesses, needs, and powerlessness. It uses its strengths to conform, achieve, and perform in an effort to prove its worth.

As we make progress on our spiritual journey, we accept the in-process nature of being human. We find freedom in the fact we were created to grow, moving *from* one level *into* a higher, more developed level *by means of* learning. We embrace learning, developing, becoming, and progressing as the pattern in all of life. Refusing to become comfortable and complacent, settling for the mediocrity of "as best I can," we pursue learning and growth. The boredom that grows out of repeated sameness is displaced by exploration and discovery. We intentionally break out of comfort zones to experience the adventure of the new.

This perspective allows us to deal with our limitations, weaknesses, and needs differently. We no longer fear them or view them as evidence that we are flawed, no good, and unlovable. Rather, we view them as arenas for continuing growth. We move beyond our fear of failure, embracing failure as yet another opportunity to learn and grow. Grace and forgiveness free us from the guilt and shame that failure generally triggers. Moving beyond the power of shame, our experiences of failure become but another opportunity for learning and growth.

Living with Confident Humility

Embracing our humanness also allows us to view and use our strengths differently.

Living out of the constructed, ego-based self, we use our abilities in self-serving ways. We use our abilities to gain attention, acceptance, affection, achievement, appreciation, and applause.

As we make progress on the journey, we learn to use our power differently. We move beyond the patterns we learned in the land of the giants. We shift our focus from others to ourselves so that we can live with self-awareness. We surrender our efforts to have power over other people, attempting to control what they think and do. Instead, we recognize the only real power we have is over ourselves. Thus, we seek to be self-responsible, using our power to manage our thinking, our emotions, and our automatic reactions. We live with integrity as deeply ingrained principles and truth guide how we choose to respond to others and to life's events.

We also recognize the specific strengths and abilities, interests and passions that have been given to us. We joyfully embrace them both as an essential part of who we are and as what we have to contribute to the world. We live with *confident humility. Confident* speaks of the strength that comes from knowing my gifts and abilities, my interests and passions, my knowledge and experience. It means I know who I am and what I have to offer to others. *Humility* speaks of the spirit behind this confidence. Humility, unlike arrogance, is not about comparing and competing. We understand our gifts and abilities do not make us better than others. They are gifts, not personal accomplishments. Humility is the recognition that all we are and all we have to share is a gift from God. The only thing about which we can boast is the generosity and grace of God.

Confident humility stands in contrast to two common attitudes found in the constructed, ego-based self. The apostle Paul addressed these two debilitating attitudes in 1 Corinthians 12:14–26. The context is Paul's teaching about the diversity of gifts that make the body of Christ strong and effective. In the teaching, he identified two attitudes about one's gifts that cripple the body. In 12:15–20, he described the *attitude of insignificance* that compares what I have to offer to the seeming superiority of someone else's gift. In 12:21–26, he described the *attitude of arrogance* that looks down on another and says, "I don't need you or what you have to offer." Arrogance is an expression of the constructed, ego-based self's *better than-less than* thinking. Confident humility is the opposite of these two common attitudes. Confident is the opposite of the attitude of insignificance. Humility is the opposite of the attitude of arrogance. Healthy spirituality fosters confident humility.

Confident humility helps us to live with courage. Courage is not the absence of fear. It is the willingness to act in the face of fear. We refuse to live out of fear. We refuse to be intimidated, afraid to speak up or act. Confident in God's faithfulness and in who God has fashioned us to be, we are willing to share what we have to give. We dare to speak up under the guidance of the Spirit, advocating the truth we know. We speak the truth we know, not out of anger or arrogance, not attacking or defending. Rather, we practice self-differentiation, taking a principle-guided "I" statement while staying connected with the other, in an attempt to be agents of healing in the midst of brokenness and agents of peace in the midst of chaos and division.

Confident humility also helps us live with intentionality. We understand what we have to share is God's gift to us, given as a way of being a blessing to others. We were blessed to be a blessing. All was given to us to be a gift to others. It was freely given to us; we give it freely to others (Matthew 10:8). We do not use God's gifts to exalt ourselves above others. We no longer use our gifts and abilities to prove our worth or to gain others' attention, approval, applause, acceptance, appreciation, or affirmation. We no longer use our gifts and abilities to hide our limitations, weaknesses, and needs. We are now free to offer our abilities as a gift to others. Because of this Spirit-given confident humility (self-confidence), we willing offer who we are and what we can do to make a difference in the life of another in Jesus's name.[64] Our giving is filled with the compassion, grace, and forgiveness that flow out of a transformed heart.

When we live out of our gifts and passions, making a difference in the lives of others, we no longer need or seek attention, approval, applause, acceptance, appreciation, or affirmation from others. Instead, we find meaning and purpose for our lives in using our gifts and experience to make a difference in the life of another.

The true self embraces our humanness, both its strengths and weaknesses. Consequently, it lives with confident humility, giving freely to others what it has to share.

A Guide for Personal Reflection and Journaling, for Group Conversation and Discussion

- What about being human is distasteful to you? What part creates pain or stirs frustration for you?
- Which focus is most characteristic of you: accomplishing, producing, and measuring up *or* learning, developing, growing, and becoming?
- What are the strengths and abilities you identify in yourself?
- Identify how you have used your strengths to gain attention, approval, applause, acceptance, appreciation, or affirmation from others.
- Identify how you have used your strengths to help others.
- Which attitude is most characteristic of you: attitude of insignificance, attitude of arrogance, or attitude of confident humility? How is that attitude expressed in your life?

CHAPTER 24
MEANINGFUL RELATIONSHIPS

We were created for relationship. Our emotional DNA programs us for togetherness. But relationships create a bind for us emotionally. We hunger for the connection and closeness for which we were created. We long to know and be known. Our sense of belonging, safeness, and value lies in those connections. At the same time, we fear being known. We are afraid if the other really knew us, they would reject us. We fear the very thing we want and need.

This emotional bind creates our dilemma: how do we meet our need to connect with others without allowing them to really know us? How do we live in relationship without running the risk of being hurt? The answer to our dilemma lies in bridges.[65]

A bridge is something we use to connect to the other. It is something we have in common: a common relationship, a common interest, a common experience, a common political position, a common religious belief, or a common hobby. Such bridges allow us to connect with the other without running the risk of being known too personally. They allow us to have the appearance of being in a relationship without the risks inherent to relationships.

As with all shortcuts, bridges leave something out. They bypass vulnerability, the heart of meaningful, close relationships. Consequently, bridges leave us wanting. They provide a surface relationship that does not speak to our deep hunger to know and be known. The relationship is not threatening, but neither is it fulfilling. It often leaves us feeling lonely and alone.

Vulnerability: The Secret to Meaningful, Close Relationships

Bridges are an inescapable part of relationships. They are a nonthreatening means of connecting. But they cannot produce deep, meaningful relationships. Meaningful relationships require something other than bridges. Meaningful relationships are cultivated through running the risk of being vulnerable. Vulnerability is the heart of meaningful, close relationships.

Vulnerability is the willingness to allow another person to know us beyond a surface level. It involves risk, so discernment is called for. Jesus instructed, "Do not give what is holy to dogs; and do not throw your pearls before swine" (Matthew 7:6). Dogs cannot value what is holy. To a dog, the holy is just like anything else. Swine cannot recognize the value of a pearl. To them, a pearl is just another stone. Jesus's words teach us to be discerning with whom we share the precious parts of our lives. They do not instruct us to *not* share them. We are to be discerning *with whom* we share them. Because being vulnerable involves risk, it requires us to trust the one with whom we share ourselves.

Vulnerability, allowing another to know us, is tied to the level at which we communicate. I identify six possible levels of communication.[66] Each successive level involves a deeper level of self-revelation.

> Level 1 – We engage in *clichés*. Level 1 acknowledges the other but involves no self-revelation by either person. At this level, we greet one another, talk about the weather, and engage in chitchat. "Hi. How are you?" (But don't really tell me!)

> Level 2 – We discuss *points of common interest*. These common interests are the bridges we use to connect. We exchange information and discuss facts. We talk about common experiences. For example, we talk about our favorite sports team or our hobbies. No self-revelation takes place.

<u>Level 3</u> – We express our *thoughts and opinions*. We reveal what we believe. This level is the first level of any degree of self-revelation. If someone disagrees with us or challenges what we believe, we will likely withdraw from the relationship.[67] If we do not withdraw from the relationship, we will keep the communication on a surface level. We do not risk any further self-revelation. Agreement becomes a prerequisite for continued relationship.

<u>Level 4</u> – We share our *feelings*, what we are feeling and why. Our feelings fall into four broad categories: mad, glad, sad, and afraid (anger, happiness, grief, and fear). Our thoughts and opinions (level 3) are often shaped more by the underlying feelings than by rational thought.

Feelings point beyond themselves to a deeper, emotional need. Feelings are like gauges on a car's dashboard whose purpose is to make us aware of something more. Our experience of anger or fear indicates a threat to one of our basic needs.

When we share our feelings, we often feel exposed. We are afraid people will use our feelings to manipulate us.

<u>Level 5</u> – We reveal our *needs*: the need to be safe, to belong, to have a sense of power and ability, or to have a sense of value and significance. Communication on this level is deeply personal and revealing.

<u>Level 6</u> – Intimacy: the freedom to know and be known.

The depth of the relationship is determined by the level at which both of us share. Such relationships are built on trust as we are willing to risk allowing the other to know us as they are willing for us to know them. (Meaningful relationships are always a two-way street: knowing and being known.) These kinds of relationships are free from judgment and criticism as any kind of censor robs the relationship of its safeness. We respect and delight in one another, treasuring the friendship. Being secure in the relationship frees us to share on any of the six levels, flowing effortlessly between them. Relationships built on this kind of vulnerability are not affected by distance or time. There is a timeless quality about them.

Because it is based on performance and appearances, the constructed, ego-based self lives with surface relationships, built with bridges. It struggles to experience the kind of relationships described here. How can we connect with one another when we are hiding behind facades and personas? But the more we grow emotionally-relationally-spiritually, the more we can move beyond surface relationships. We are free to explore deeper, more meaningful relationships.

Meaningful relationships are built with healthy boundaries. They are possible as each person is self-aware, self-managing, and self-responsible. They are not necessarily free from struggle, but exercising self-differentiation transforms the difficulties into deeper trust and greater freedom.

Because vulnerability is the secret to meaningful relationships, using "I" statements is vital. "I" statements indicate I am attempting to maintain healthy boundaries and be self-responsible. They communicate what I am thinking, feeling, and wanting, allowing the other to know me. "You" statements, on the other hand, are consciously avoided. "You" statements express judgment and blame, robbing the relationship of safeness. Without safeness, vulnerability is not possible. Without vulnerability, meaningful relationships are not possible.

Deep, meaningful relationships, like using our gifts and abilities to make a difference in the life of another, are one of the sources to the richness of life. They are a dimension of the life of the true self.

A Guide for Personal Reflection and Journaling, for Group Conversation and Discussion

- Review the six levels of communication in relationship to your normal relationships. At what level do you relate?
- What bridges do you most commonly use to build relationships?
- What obstacles do you recognize within yourself to building deeper relationships?
- Identify those who knows you best .

CHAPTER 25
PEACE, JOY, AND THANKSGIVING

Is the glass half full or half empty?

This question is often used to describe whether we are an optimist or a pessimist, whether we live with a positive disposition or a negative one. The question implies our inner disposition is a dimension of personality. And to some degree, it probably is. But our inner strength also factors into the emotional tone out of which we live.

Our emotional tone is governed by what is in our hearts and minds. So as we mature emotionally-relationally-spiritually, as the Spirit transforms what is in our heart, as we learn to use our power to manage ourselves, the emotional tone out of which we live is transformed as well.

The emotional tone out of which the constructed, ego-based self lives is governed by anxiety and fear. These two underlie whatever disposition is presented on the surface. The spiritual journey leads us into the healing of the emotional wounds from which anxiety and fear arise. On the journey, we learn to recognize them when they surface (self-awareness) and manage them so that they no longer have power (self-management). We learn how to move beyond them and their power. At the same time, we learn how to live in peace. We learn how to place ourselves in a position for the Spirit to guide us into the peace of Christ. Peace displaces the anxiety and fear. When peace is what is in our hearts, how we view and respond to others changes. We become more patient, kind, generous, faithful, and gentle in how we treat others.[68]

As we make progress on the journey, accessing God's peace becomes a pattern with which we live. Inner strength develops as we become more

129

self-confident in using our power to manage ourselves. Peace becomes the posture from which we live.

Peace makes a way for joy to flow.

The constructed, ego-based self knows very little about joy. Its focus on measuring up and achieving keeps anxiety stirred up. Its focus on others and attempts to control what others think, feel, and do keeps it stuck in anxiety. It lives with the frustration of being unable to get others to do what it wants. The feeling of being powerless fuels the anxiety. Consequently, the constructed, ego-based self turns to entertainment and excitement, stimulation and pleasure to fill the void left by the absence of joy.

Joy is the response of the heart to God's grace and goodness. Joy opens our eyes to the giftedness and goodness of life. We begin to recognize the gifts of creation, testimonies of God's presence and love. We rejoice in seeing God's work around us. We treasure meaningful relationships as a dimension of life's richness. Some of our greatest experiences of joy come in the sharing of our gifts to make a difference in the lives of others. We find joy in our emotional-relational-spiritual growth. We experience joy as we share our journey with others on the journey. We find joy in the progress and healing of others as they discover and live into God's grace. Joy, rooted in peace, becomes the emotional tone out of which we live. We experience it as delight in another, in an experience, and in our lives.

Joy in God's grace and goodness gives birth to thanksgiving. Thanksgiving is more than gratitude for a particular gift or experience. It is the recognition and acknowledgment that all of life is a gift. Thanksgiving moves us beyond the gift to the Source of the gift. It leads us back to God. It trains us to live out of deep faith in and glad dependency on God's faithfulness.

What is on the inside is expressed in what is on the outside. As peace, joy, and thanksgiving become the emotional tone out of which we live, we begin to live out of joyous generosity. The anxiety-based scarcity thinking of the constructed, ego-based self is displaced by the generosity of God and abundance of the kingdom. Giving is viewed as an investment that pays a huge return and as planting that produces an abundant harvest (2 Corinthians 9:6–10). It becomes a way of life. Joyous generosity becomes a part of everything we do.

Peace, joy, and thanksgiving are the emotional tone of the true self. They lead to and are expressed in joyous generosity.

A Guide for Personal Reflection and Journaling, for Group Conversation and Discussion

- How would you describe your normal emotional tone? How would others describe your emotional tone?
- How would you describe your normal emotional tone under stress or in crisis?
- How has your emotional tone changed during your lifetime?
- What do you do (or could you do) to cultivate peace, joy, and thanksgiving as the emotional tone out of which you live?

CHAPTER 26
COUNT IT ALL JOY: DEALING DIFFERENTLY WITH PAIN AND SUFFERING

Pain and suffering, chaos and uncertainty are inescapable realities of life. Sometimes, we create our own chaos and pain by the choices we make. Sometimes, our chaos and pain are the result of someone else's choices. Sometimes, chaos and pain just are. Stuff happens. We live in a seemingly broken world. The apostle Paul spoke of this reality when he described creation as being in "bondage to decay" (Romans 8:21). Consequently, life's experiences are often hard and harsh, full of challenge. We cannot avoid pain and suffering, chaos and uncertainty. We have to deal with them.

Pain and suffering, chaos and uncertainty contribute to the anxiety with which we live. We often get trapped in anticipation of "What would happen if …?" Our minds are quick to fear the worst. We seek to protect ourselves from what might happen. We live with fear of what might happen to our children. We fear growing old and becoming debilitated. Older adults fear losing independence. The thought of being confined to a wheel chair or a long-term care facility is terrifying. They fear losing awareness to dementia or Alzheimer's. And of course, we fear death.

All of these things we fear are not current threats to which we can respond. They are things we anticipate and manufacture with our thinking. They are things that add to our anxiety and cause us to worry. We fear them and what they will do to us. We are anxious we will not have the resources or ability to deal with what comes our way.

But then, the things we fear become reality. We find ourselves dealing with the challenges of pain and suffering, of chaos and uncertainty. The stuff that happens is happening to us!

One of the determining factors in what we experience, often overlooked or unrecognized, is not the experience itself but *our response* to it. How we respond (or react) contributes to the impact the challenge has on us. Our response determines what the long-term impact will be.

How we respond to a challenge, in turn, is determined by our degree of anxiety and fear about the situation. And our anxiety and fear are directly tied to our sense of power and control.

Our sense of power to deal with a situation is what distinguishes a problem from a crisis. A problem is a situation that is difficult, but we have the abilities and resources to deal with it. We feel some sense of control. A crisis is a situation in which we feel powerless and out of control. Being powerless or out of control is one of our greatest fears.

Our sense of power and control determines our level of anxiety. Our level of anxiety governs our response to the situation. Our response determines the impact of the situation.

The wisdom of the biblical writers calls for a strange response to pain and suffering. "We boast in our sufferings" (Romans 5:3). "Whenever you face trials of any kind, consider it nothing but joy" (James 1:2). "Rejoice always. Give thanks in all circumstances" (1 Thessalonians 5:16, 18). "Rejoice in the Lord always! Do not worry about anything" (Philippians 4:4, 6).

Such exhortations are challenging, if not downright impossible. Our normal reaction is to fear the challenge. Anxiety and worry fill our hearts and minds. We want to escape the challenge and its pain as quickly as possible. We want someone to fix what's wrong so we can get on with our lives. We pray the surgery or the chemo works. Fear and anxiety consume us and dictate how we respond.

The biblical exhortations call us to view the pain and suffering, chaos and uncertainty differently. Instead of reacting out of anxiety and fear, the biblical writers call us to respond to them with joy and thanksgiving, even to the point of boasting in them! Embracing this inner disposition calls us beyond the anxiety that permeates such situations. It frees us to respond differently.

Exhortations are commands. They engage thinking and the will. Being self-aware and self-managing also engage thinking and the will. The exhortations call us beyond emotion (anxiety and fear, anger and angst) to think clearly. Such is possible through self-awareness. Being aware of our inner anxiety calls us to manage the anxiety, moving beyond it into peace where we can think clearly.[69] Thinking allows us to choose how to respond rather than being controlled by automatic, fear-driven reactions (self-management).

Being self-aware and self-managing gives us a sense of power in the face of a situation in which we feel powerless. They place us in a position to experience the Spirit's peace in the face of uncertainty and threat. Being self-aware and self-managing position us to adopt a disposition colored by joy and thanksgiving. The joy and thanksgiving are not *for* the situation but *in* the situation.

Responding with joy and thanksgiving to pain and suffering, chaos and uncertainty is an expression of faith. Faith fuels the exhortations. Paul's exhortation "Rejoice in the Lord always!" is paired with the reassurance "The Lord is near!" (Philippians 4:5). Paul reassures his readers of God's presence with them, walking with them through the situation and supplying what they need for it.[70] His words about boasting in sufferings are grounded in his assurance.

> *Knowing* that suffering produces endurance and endurance produces character and character produces hope and hope does not disappoint us, because God's love has been poured into our hearts through the Holy Spirit that has been given to us. (Romans 5:3–5; emphasis added)

Paul understood how God transforms the challenges and struggles of life into emotional relational-spiritual growth. The strength to endure only comes through trial (suffering). Enduring the trial allows character to develop. Such growth reassures us of God's promise to mature us into the likeness of Christ (hope). The writer of James expressed the same thinking. "Whenever you face trials of any kind, consider it nothing but joy *because you know* that the testing of your faith produces endurance, and let endurance have its full effect so that you may be mature and complete, lacking nothing" (James 1:2–4; emphasis added).

This kind of Spirit-empowered response to chaos and suffering expresses faith in God's presence with us in the midst of the experience. It expresses faith that God's presence will provide us strength beyond our own to deal with the challenge. It expresses faith in God's provision of peace in the midst of it, through the exercise of self-awareness and self-management (Philippians 4:4–7). A response of thanksgiving and joy expresses faith in God's work to sustain us in the midst of the challenge. It expresses faith in God's promise to work in the challenge, transforming it into a crucible of growth in our becoming like Christ.

A response of thanksgiving and joy is foreign to the constructed, ego-based self. But it is possible as we make progress on our spiritual journey and the true self emerges.

Facing the Reality of Death

As we make progress on the journey, we see and respond to the experiences of life differently. The spiritual truths the Spirit teaches us train us to live out of a perspective free from the sabotaging power of anxiety. Progress also leads us to see and respond differently to the reality of death.

The fear of death is a normal part of our human experience. We never feel more powerless than when facing the reality of death. (Being powerless is one of our greatest fears.)

Death represents the end. It speaks of the end of our life, the end of who we are. Death represents loss. It speaks of the loss of those we love, the loss of all we have gained. And we are powerless to avoid it. No wonder we fear death!

Progress on our spiritual journey leads us to view death differently. We move beyond our fear of death.

Rather than viewing death as the end and as loss, we view death as a transition. The apostle Paul expressed this perspective to the Philippian church as he wrote to them about his impending death. He used two images to speak of death as a transition rather than an end.

> For to me, living is Christ and dying is gain. If I am to
> live in the flesh, that means fruitful labor for me; and I do
> not know which I prefer. I am hard pressed between the
> two: my desire is to depart and be with Christ, for that is
> far better; but to remain in the flesh is more necessary for
> you. (Philippians 1:21–24)

Paul spoke of dying as *gain*. The word he used is a financial term similar to our concept of dividends paid out. He did not view death as a loss but rather as a return on an investment. He would continue to experience what he had experienced in life: living in relationship with the Risen Christ, sharing his life. But his experience beyond death would be a greater experience of that life. His experience of living in relationship with the Risen Christ and sharing Christ's life was the principle. Dying would add the dividends the principle paid out. It would be Christ's life plus! Death was a transition to a greater experience of what he had already experienced in his relationship with God.

The second image Paul used was a sailing term. "My desire is to depart." The word *depart* meant to cast off the ropes that held the ship to the dock, setting it free to sail. Paul's thought was death was a casting off from this shore (life) and setting sail for another destination. It was not a loss but a setting off to the next port of call and all that it held.

Of course, Paul commonly spoke of death in relationship with resurrection: death and resurrection. He understood the new life of resurrection was only possible through death. Death always gave way to resurrection. It gave way to new life through the power of the Risen Christ. Paul spoke of death and resurrection as the pattern of Christ's life in which we participate.[71] He used the image in relation to how we live as well as in relation to how we face death. Death was a passage into greater life.[72]

One of my favorite images of death is the experience of birth. When a child is in utero, her every need is met by her mother. She floats in a safe, comfortable world. She is comforted by the familiar rhythm of her mother's breathing and heartbeat. But when the time for her delivery comes, her safe, comfortable world comes to an end. The comfort of the water in which she has floated is suddenly gone. Her mother's breathing and heartbeat become rapid and unfamiliar. Her mother's body begins to forcibly push her down through an unfamiliar, constricted passage. Her life as she has known it is coming to an end. She is losing everything with which she is familiar. If she could think and speak, she would say she was dying. But on the other side of that passage are people who are eagerly and joyfully anticipating her arrival. They speak of her arrival as birth, the beginning of her life. From one perspective, the experience is viewed as death. From another, the same experience is viewed as birth. Both perspectives are real. Her experience is death to one stage of life: life in utero. Her experience is also birth, the entrance into a new stage of life. Her birth experience is a transition from one dimension of life to the next. She is moving *from, into.* Our faith in God's grace and faithfulness leads us to view our physical death as a transition from one dimension of life to the next, fuller stage.

Progress on the journey teaches us to view death as a transition. It is the means by which we move to a fuller, deeper experience of God and God's life that we have known on our journey here. It is not a loss but dividends paid out. It is not an end but a new beginning. Death is a transition to a deeper, fuller experience of the life in Christ that we have experienced in this world.

Our journey of emotional-relational-spiritual growth continues beyond what we call death. God created us with unlimited capacity for growth. It will take eternity to exhaust the potential God has placed within us. So there is no end to the Spirit's transforming, maturing work in our life. The journey with God is eternal. Yet the outcome is guaranteed: we will be fully conformed to the likeness of Christ. The writer of the New Testament book of Ephesians expressed it this way: "until all of us come … to maturity, to the measure of the full stature of Christ" (Ephesians 4:13).

Death is but our next step on this spiritual journey, a transition to the next stage. Through it we move *from, into.*

A Guide for Personal Reflection and Journaling, for Group Conversation and Discussion

- Recall an experience of personal crisis. How did you react during it? What helped you deal with it and get through it?
- Where did you see or experience God in it?

- What did you learn from the experience? How did it change you?
- What do you need in order to live out of joy and thanksgiving in the midst of a crisis?
- How would you describe your attitude about death and dying?
- What metaphor captures the spirit of your attitude about death and dying?

CHAPTER 27
OUT OF STEP, AGAINST THE GRAIN

The constructed, ego-based self reflects our culture. It embodies the thinking and values of our society.

Our culture is a merit-based culture. The principle of earning-deserving drives its thinking. Consequently, it deals in rewards and punishments doled out according to how one measures up. Power is not equally distributed within our culture, which means the rewards and punishments are not always equitable. Those in power often use it against others for their own advantage. Our culture is built upon achieving and accomplishing. Doing is valued over enrichment. Work is valued over relationships. Our culture is permeated with *us-them* thinking and relating. It is segregated into multiple, competing expressions of "those like us." It feeds on competition. Each different group considers itself to be right. We struggle to accept, much less respect, those who are different. We consider our group to be *better than* others and others to be *less than* our group. Our merit-based culture is a highly polarized culture.

Like the constructed, ego-based self, our culture is driven by anxiety. Every organization, institution, group, and workplace is an emotional system floating on a sea of anxiety. Every member within those organizations, institutions, and workplaces reads the system and the others in the system through the lens of anxiety. Each one subconsciously functions on high alert, seeking to identify any potential threat to their having a safe place or being valued or being capable in the system. The anxiety of the individual person contributes to the pool of anxiety in the group. The anxiety of the group contributes to the anxiety permeating society.[73]

As we make progress on our journey, growing emotionally-relationally-spiritually, we not only begin to move beyond our constructed, ego-based self with its merit-based thinking, we also begin to be out of step with the culture in which we live. We see things from a different perspective. Our thinking goes against the flow of culture. Our values cut across the grain of society. Who we have become is at odds with who the world shaped us to be.

Being different and out of step is isolating. It goes against our fundamental need to live in relationship (the togetherness force). Going against the grain stirs the anxiety associated with our basic emotional needs. It was that anxiety that fueled the construction of our constructed, ego-based self in the first place. Thus, finding another source for our togetherness-relational needs is essential. Those needs are addressed by spiritual friends and a spiritual community.

Meaningful relationships with like-minded, spiritual friends are an important resource for our journey. We connect with others who are walking the journey and pursuing emotional-relational-spiritual growth. I have found three levels of relationships to be valuable. First, we cultivate a spiritual friend who is our companion on the journey or we turn to a spiritual guide, counselor, or coach. In addition, we develop a small group of trusted spiritual friends with whom we share the journey, to whom we turn with our struggles, and with whom we pray. We see this pattern in Jesus's life as he turned to Peter, James, and John as his inner circle. Finally, we are a part of a larger spiritual community that focuses on the journey and nurtures emotional-relational-spiritual growth. These resources help us stay grounded in our thinking. They encourage us as we struggle and face challenges. They celebrate with us our progress and growth. They affirm who we are and the gifts we have to offer. They provide guidance and support as we walk our journey.

Vital support for the journey of *Discovering Your True Self* is found in such spiritually-oriented relationships.

A Guide for Personal Reflection and Journaling, for Group Conversation and Discussion

- Identify areas of your life in which you are out of step with the culture in which you live.
- What stress or anxiety does being out of step cause you? What resources do you use to deal with it?
- Who is your spiritual companion? Who is in your spiritual small group? What is your spiritual community?
- What do you draw from these resources that help you on your journey?
- What do you do to cultivate these relationships?

EPILOGUE

I have sought to describe a journey of emotional-relational-spiritual growth that leads to *Discovering Your True Self*. For me, this journey is the very essence of life.

The journey begins as we identify the anxiety-driven, merit-based thinking that drives us to construct a public persona patterned after who the world says we should be. Our journey leads us beyond this constructed, ego-based self (*from*). The goal of the journey is emotional-relational-spiritual maturity that sets the true self free (*into*). It results in the beauty of God's character being expressed through the beauty and uniqueness of our individual personalities. The core of the journey is the renewing of the mind and transformation of the heart (*by means of*). Relational tools, such as healthy boundaries and being self-aware, self-managing, and self-responsible, help bring the transformation into reality. As we make progress on this journey, we view and experience life differently. We move beyond the sabotaging power of anxiety. We move beyond the shame that is the poison of merit-based thinking. We embrace our humanness, living with confident humility. We find meaning and purpose by using our gifts and abilities to make a difference in the life of another. We enjoy the richness of deep, meaningful relationships. We live with joy, peace, and thanksgiving, freeing us to give with joyous generosity. We embrace the challenges and crises of life with faith as an occasion for God's work of maturing us into the likeness of Christ.

In outlining this journey, I do not mean to imply I have moved beyond the sabotaging power of anxiety. I am not claiming to have arrived. I am still very much "in process." By the grace of God, I have made some progress. I certainly am not where I once was, thanks be to God! But I am far from where the journey will take me.

The truth is the journey never ends. Our journey continues beyond death as the Spirit continues to recreate us in God's likeness and set our true self free.

As long as we are in this world, our journey will involve struggle. We never escape the presence of anxiety in our lives. We never completely escape our old issues, the merit-based stinking thinking that fuels them, or our old patterns. We can easily revert back to our old ways of thinking and relating.

Merit-based, stinking thinking is deeply ingrained. In addition, it is reinforced by the culture in which we live. Its power does not automatically dissipate as we learn the truth and ways of God. It is resilient, quietly resurfacing when something pushes our button and triggers our old issues. The old messages begin to play again, often outside our conscious awareness, pulling us back into old patterns, stirring old feelings of defeat and self-reproach. We get stuck again, trapped in old, merit-based thinking.

Such experiences are normal. More importantly, they are an opportunity for growth! Recognizing the old thoughts, feelings, and patterns (self-awareness) becomes an opportunity to practice self-management. We engage in breath prayer and/or meditation to move back into God's peace. We remember and reclaim the truths that offset the stinking thinking. We once again move *from* the old *into* the new *by means of* thinking from a different, God-shaped perspective. What on the surface looks like a relapse actually becomes a means of growing stronger in the new way of thinking. Each time we are self-aware and self-managing, we become stronger in these new ways of thinking and living.

As we make progress on the journey, the power of the old issues, thinking, and patterns diminishes. We recognize them more quickly and act to move beyond them. They remain a part of our past, but they no longer have the power to sabotage our present or determine our future. They are more like scars than open wounds. They become reminders of where we have been and occasions to give thanks to God for the Spirit's transforming work in our life.

The attitude of the apostle Paul, expressed to the followers of Jesus at Philippi, is a model for us to follow as we walk the journey.

Not that I have already obtained this (objective) or have already reached the goal; but I press on to make it my own, because Christ Jesus has made me his own. Beloved, ... this one thing I do: forgetting what lies behind and straining forward to what lies ahead, I press on towards the goal for the prize of the heavenly call of God in Christ Jesus. Let those of us then who are mature be of the same mind. (Philippians 3:12–15)

I press on. I keep walking the journey. I seek to stay open to the Spirit's transforming work in my life. I don't give up or quit. I press on.

I pray you too will press on. Cultivate a small circle of spiritual friends with whom to share the journey. Perhaps you could use this book as a guide for the group's sharing. Find a spiritual guide or a Bowen-trained therapist to support you on the journey. However you pursue the journey, press on.

And so the journey continues, under the direction of the Spirit.

A Guide for Personal Reflection and Journaling, for Group Conversation and Discussion

- What is your takeaway from reading this book and doing this work?
- How are you different because of your work?
- In what area do you see the need for additional growth?
- With whom will you share your story?
- What will you do to press on?

I press on.

APPENDICES

APPENDIX A

Denise's Story[74]

The training was something I was looking forward to. Although just a small part of the larger class I was taking, this training would provide the link to bridge me from the classroom into the field—from theory into practice. I was both excited and a little anxious because this link would give me the tool I needed to do the work to which I felt called. Yet my anxiety seemed to override my rational thinking by whispering into my ear, "What if you don't *get it?* What if you fail? Are you even smart enough—good enough?"

However, I reminded myself that in my experience, I have found with the right training, an effective instructor, and some obsessive note taking, I usually conquer my fears and eventually master the skill. Plus there is always a little grace 'n space for newbies like me to learn. Those thoughts took my anxiety down a notch or two. So I was ready and looking forward to the training.

A few weeks ago, on Monday morning, our instructor announced to us that that day the specialized trainer would be coming to our class to give us the training we needed in order to take the next step. We gathered in a computer lab to go through the mock program designed for the training. Our instructor hooked his computer up to the projector so his screen was visible to the class. Unfortunately, this is when the trouble began.

Our instructor spoke so rapidly that I could not take notes, pay attention to the big screen, and do the mock exercises on my screen at the same time. My anxiety began to rise. He gave instructions at double speed, and I couldn't keep up. I was embarrassed and hesitant to tell him that I was lost or that I didn't understand. I noticed my computer screen didn't look like my instructor's computer screen. Tabs and buttons were in different places, so instructions to "Click here," "Click there," "Drag this here," and "Drag that there" meant nothing to me. I was lost, frustrated, and humiliated. The instructor kept asking, "Any questions?" but the speed with which he asked and waited, and the embarrassment of still being lost and confused, became overwhelming. I put my hand up and said I was lost. He came over, looked at my screen, and said my screen was set up completely differently. "Come to the back" he said, "and watch me at my screen."

Suddenly I felt it coming like an oncoming train. I was shutting down. I gave up even trying to follow along. I gave up even trying to "Click this" or "Drag that." I just checked out. Powered down. Tears welled up, and I confirmed to myself that I just couldn't get it, that I wasn't good enough or smart enough. What was I going to do? I left the training ready to quit.

Hours later, I reflected on the experience. I remembered how many other times I had felt the same way. I had shut down and wanted to quit. Exercising as much self-awareness as I could conjure up, I realized the reaction I had is my pattern. Reviewing, I could pinpoint several circumstances in which I felt the same way. Then I asked myself, "So how did those past situations turn out?" Just fine. I powered through and thrived at each of the other situations. Looking back, I couldn't believe I even considered quitting.

I would like to say this won't happen again, that I have learned my lesson, but I've got to be realistic that it will happen again. After all, it is my pattern.

APPENDIX B

In the early hours of the morning, I had a very scary dream. There was a commotion in the backyard; I heard a raccoon squealing. I saw a huge brown dog, like a Lab but much bigger, clamp his jaws around the raccoon and pick it up, shaking his head violently. I think I squeezed my eyes shut. I opened the back door and called to my cat Leo, who seemed to be frozen. The huge dog jumped the fence. I went out to get Leo and bring him in.

Now in the house, there was a huge man with three big guns. I said something like "I didn't invite you into my house," and his answer was something like "But I'm here. I protect the neighborhood." His name was Hananiah. A short guy was with him. As Hananiah strode around the room, the little guy kept moving the guns nearer to Hananiah, keeping them in his line of sight. I'm thinking that even if I had guns accessible, I would not want to get in a gun fight with this scary man!

I began asking Hananiah questions like "Why are you so angry?" and "What or who do you see as a threat?" He kept pacing, and the little guy kept moving the guns.

The only response I remember was Hananiah beginning with "My grandmother …"

I woke up and asked, "Why such an awful dream?"

Later, as I sat in the sauna, my impression was that Hananiah was the breast cancer that has reappeared, spreading to my bones, terminal, uninvited.

I think of my friend who has lived with lung cancer fifteen years and refuses to think in violent terms such as "killing cancer." Instead she suggests to cancer cells that their time is up and mentally ushers them to the door. Like my friend, I do not choose violent images to deal with cancer.

And my grandmother had breast cancer.

I looked up Hananiah. He's one of the three with Daniel in the Hebrew scriptures. King Nebuchadnezzar's chief official renamed him Shadrach, but his Hebrew name was Hananiah, and Hananiah means "Yah is merciful."

A second wave of understanding followed: living in a God-shaped world, the kingdom teaching is affirmed yet again. Even when violence is advanced against us, our response is not violent.

"My grandmother" points to a genetic link to cancer but also to inheriting her emotional and physical response to cancer. Her responses were not fear based. She waited until they moved into town and completed the sale of household goods and the farm before she went to the city for surgery. My memory is it was about a month delay. As surely as I got her genetic imprint, I have her spirit to walk with me through cancer that will take me home.

The name Hananiah tells me that even in cancer, I will experience God's mercies. Culture and powerful people can change his name and put him in a fire, but God's mercies, Yahweh's mercies, remain in the midst of it all.

Now I might have said, "That's a horrible dream, and I'm going to push it aside until I forget it." Instead, I sat with it, watched, and listened. I began to see God's hand, feel his presence, and become confident in his offer of peace and joy in the midst of pain. The negative, scary part of the dream lost its power. All that remains is knowing in that deep, deep place that my Abba sees my heart, loves me, prepares me, and provides for me.

Thanks be to God!

If I had to choose one verse in the Bible as my verse, it is from Isaiah 30:15. "In returning and rest you shall be saved; in quietness and in trust shall be your strength." The Message paraphrase says, "Your salvation requires you to turn back to me and stop your silly efforts to save yourselves. Your strength will come from settling down in complete dependence on me."[76] I find that to be so true.

APPENDIX C

Symptoms of the Constructed Self Syndrome in Religious Life[77]

Religious practices often get co-opted by the constructed, ego-based self. When they do, the church becomes an arena for the constructed, ego-based self, dressed in religious garb, to live out its identity. The church suffers from the constructed self syndrome. The symptoms are predictable.

- Some standard of measurement (unstated expectations) permeates everything. It may be proper belief (about the Bible, about sin, about God), proper behavior (morals or "reverence in worship" or mission support), or proper ritual (the right way to worship). Rules and policies (what we can do, can't do) govern the life of the church.
- Conformity—doing the right things in the right way—is expected. Thus, a spirit of performance, particularly in worship, creeps in. Appearances are important as are meeting expectations of what people want or like.
- A reserved sense of evaluation is the prevailing emotional tone. Criticism and complaint, judgment and condemnation are often expressed about failure to measure up to expectations. Criticism and complaint, judgment and condemnation become power plays to control what happens and how. This spirit of judgment excludes any sense of joy or expression of creativity.
- Acceptance and approval are conditional, tied to how well one conforms to the expectations and norms. The congregation struggles to offer God's kind of radical hospitality.

- An *us-them* spirit is the norm. Belonging is limited to those like us—who think like us, look like us, act like us, and value what we value. Those not like us are often targeted for condemnation as unacceptable, undesirable, less-than, or even, sinful.
- Relationships tend to be more social than spiritual. We enjoy being together and find ways to do so, but we seldom share honestly of our spiritual struggles.
- Leadership is restricted to those who are committed to the way we do things. Leaders function as managers protecting and maintaining the status quo.
- We openly express pride about our past. We often speak of "the good old days." We continue to do what we have always done and how we have always done it, assuming it is what is pleasing to God—because it is pleasing to us! There is little hunger for "more" spiritually.
- Clinging to what we have always done and how we have always done it, we resist anything new or different, anything that disrupts the comfort zones we have created for ourselves (i.e., change). We interpret the introduction of change as criticism, meaning we're doing it wrong.
- We ask God to bless what we are doing rather than ask how we can be a part of what God is doing.

When church life becomes infected with the constructed self syndrome, it becomes a reflection of the culture rather than a reflection of God. It dresses the world's ways in religious garb rather than embodying the ways of God (the kingdom). It uses God to validate who we are and what we do rather than allowing God to shape who we are and what we do.

The constructed self syndrome is a never-ending battle in church life. Its only antidote is healthy spirituality.

APPENDIX D

Grace-Based versus Merit-Based Religious Life

<u>Initiative or First Step</u>

Grace based: God *initiates*; I respond. God's grace elicits a response of faith. Grace-faith.

Merit based: I *initiate*, taking the first step; God responds. If I will …, then God will. Earning-deserving, merit-reward thinking

<u>Emphasis</u>

Grace based: The *emphasis* is upon relationship with God and growing through that relationship.

Merit based: The *emphasis* is upon measuring up to expectations and demands expressed in a code of ethics or beliefs. Law.

<u>Rooted in</u>

Grace based: Everything is *rooted in* and grows out of the personal relationship with God, empowered by the Spirit. Marked by glad dependency upon the Spirit.

Merit based: Everything is *rooted in* and depends upon self-effort and self-reliance.

Focus

Grace based: The *focus* is the heart, the interior realm. This focus results in authenticity.

Merit based: The *focus* is behavior, the external realm. This focus results in appearances and pretense.

Goal

Grace based: The *goal* is the transformation of heart and life—spiritual growth.

Merit based: The *goal* is conformity of belief, behavior, and ritual—outward appearance.

Tone

Grace based: The *tone* is unconditional. Acceptance and forgiveness are gifts freely given.

Merit based: The *tone* is conditional. Acceptance is based on conformity. Forgiveness is based on repentance. We get what we deserve.

Power

Grace based: *Power* is used to serve, to empower others, to nurture and bless.

Merit based: *Power* is used to control and dominate others, to reward those who conform and to punish those who do not; to manipulate.

Produces

Grace based: Grace produces *love and gratitude* expressed in praise and thanksgiving.

Merit based: Merit-based relating produces and plays on *guilt and fear*.

Reward

Grace based: The *reward* is God's kind of life (eternal life) here and now as well as after death.

Merit based: Merit-based relating deals in *rewards and punishment,* including acceptance and rejection now and heaven and hell after death.

Scripture

Grace based: *Scripture* is viewed and used as the record of God's self-revelation in Jesus of Nazareth.

Merit based: *Scripture* is viewed as the authoritative word of God, having absolute authority regarding proper belief, behavior, and ritual.

The Church

Grace based: The *church* is an inclusive, nurturing community in which all are valued and embraced as God's children. It expresses the radical hospitality of God.

Merit based: The *church* is an exclusive community functioning out of an *us-them* mentality. It is for those like us in belief, behavior, and ritual. Uniformity is valued over diversity.

Outcome

Grace based: Kingdom of God.
Merit based: Religion.

APPENDIX E

Triangles: The Geometry of Relationships

Our lives are made rich by healthy, meaningful relationships. But relationships entail one of life's most challenging realities. BFST uses the concept of triangles to describe the anxiety-driven dynamics of relationships. Understanding triangles is another tool that can help us move toward healthier, more meaningful relationships. It is a valuable companion to living with healthy emotional boundaries and to being self-aware, self-managing, and self-responsible.

BFST speaks of triangles as the basic build blocks of relationships. They are not good or bad. They just are. And they are inescapable. They are a reality in every relationship.

Triangles as Anxiety Binders

Triangles grow out of and are an attempt to manage the anxiety that is inherent in relationships, particularly the anxiety about being known. The fear of being known (being vulnerable) makes a two-person relationship the most unstable of relationships. Anxiety grows as we become more vulnerable. The more vulnerability we experience, the more anxious we become. We escape the anxiety by creating a triangle. We move away from knowing and being known to talking about something less threatening. We shift the focus from the two of us to someone or something outside us. We stop talking about ourselves and begin to talk about someone or something besides us. Couples talk about the kids and schedules. Friends talk about the upcoming game or the concert they attended or the movie they saw. Coworkers talk about work or coworkers or the boss. The most common thing we talk about is another person, particularly something negative about them. A common enemy makes good allies.

Triangles are an avoidance mechanism. They allow us to build a bridge to another person without allowing them to really know us. They allow us to avoid the anxiety of being known.

How Triangles Function

Triangles have three components, represented by the three corners of the triangle. The three components are the two persons involved in the relationship (A and B) and the bridge they use to connect (C). C may be a person, such as a child or parent or coworker or friend, or something the two have in common. In BFST, the third corner of the triangle is always another person, but the principle works with something other than a person.

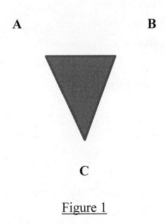

Figure 1

In every triangle, two of the corners are considered the inside position (A and B). The other is in an outside position (C). See figure 1. A and B are drawn closer together while C is drawn apart from them.

When the triangle involves three people (A, B, and C), the two inside positions are generally the comfortable positions (A and B). They enjoy the benefits of being connected. Their need to belong is being met so their anxiety is low. However, the belonging need of the person in the outside position (C) is not being met. Thus, person C experiences a higher level of anxiety. In an effort to lower their anxiety, the person in the outside position (C) seeks to connect with one of the other two individuals, moving to an inside position with that one (A). Their move displaces the third person (B) into the uncomfortable outside position. Compare figure 2.

A   **B**

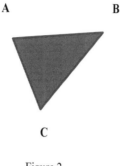

C

<u>Figure 2</u>

This kind of shifting generally occurs repeatedly and subconsciously.

An exception to this pattern is when the two in the inside positions are in conflict. Then, the comfortable position is the outside position, outside of the conflict. Invariably, however, one of the two who are in conflict (A) will seek to establish an inside position with the outsider (C), enlisting them as an ally in the conflict. The alliance places the other person (B) in the outside position. Now A and C are aligned against B in the conflict. The relationships in the triangle have shifted.

Triangles and Boundaries

Triangles reflect boundary violations and a failure to be self-responsible. In the functioning of a triangle, the focus is on the other two persons, not on self. Self-awareness is not being exercised. Without self-awareness, self-management cannot occur. Instead, power is used to influence the relationships in the triangle, not to manage self.

Triangles can be used to map boundary violations. In chapter 7, we met Diana, who nagged her husband in an effort to get him to stop drinking. The three corners of this triangle are Diana, her husband, and her husband's drinking. The responsibility for her husband's drinking belongs to the husband. The husband and his drinking should be the two inside corners. But Diana functions with a lack of healthy boundaries, robbing him of the responsibility. Diana and her husband's drinking are the two inside corners; her husband is in the outside corner. See figure 3.

Diana   **Husband**

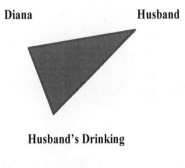

Husband's Drinking

Figure 3

Diana's efforts actually have the opposite effect to what she intended. Her nagging about his drinking contributed to him drinking more. Diana's example illustrates another truth about triangles: any attempt to change the triangle will backfire, producing the opposite effect. As long as Diana assumed responsibility for her husband's drinking, he did not have to assume any responsibility for it. He could only take responsibility for his drinking when Diana released it. Diana's example can apply to any relationship in which one person assumes responsibility for what belongs to another (e.g., a parent with a child's homework or room, a supervisor with an employee's habitual tardiness, a pastor with her parishioners' beliefs or behavior, and couples in a conflict). Drawing a triangle graphically depicts how responsibility has been displaced.

The only way to change the dynamics of a triangle is to change how *we* function in it. If Diana changed her functioning (i.e., gave up her attempts to get her husband to quit drinking), then he would have to deal with his drinking. She could change her functioning by taking a principled, self-differentiated "I" position. See figure 4. Diana has placed herself in the outside corner.

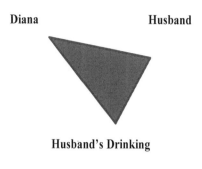

Diana   Husband

Husband's Drinking

Figure 4

We can change the way we function in triangles by being self-aware, self-managing, and self-responsible. Rather than continue to participate in the shifting positions, we can consciously choose to place ourselves in what is called a neutral corner. The neutral corner is the outside position with different functioning. From this outside or neutral position, we maintain connection with both of the other two individuals. Taking the neutral corner involves an act of self-differentiation: taking a principled "I" position while staying connected with the other. Assuming the neutral corner prevents us from taking an inside position with one, thereby putting the other in the outside corner.

We cannot escape the dynamics of a relational triangle. We can, however, understand them and use them as a guide to healthier functioning. They can be a tool to foster self-awareness and self-management.

Interlocking Triangles: How Groups Are Connected

Triangles are not just found in two-party relationships. In any group, everyone is connected to everyone else through a series of interlocking triangles. We may not have a one-on-one connection with every person in the group, but we have a one-on-one connection with someone who does have a one-on-one connection with the other. A unit supervisor has a one-on-one relationship with every one of her people. But she does not personally know everyone who works for her people in support roles. She is connected to the support personnel through the people she supervises.

They are all interconnected, just not through one-on-one relationships. They are connected through a series of interlocking triangles.

This interconnection is a factor in how the group is affected by anxiety. Anxiety flows throughout the group (what BFST calls an emotional system) through these interlocking triangles. What stirs anxiety in one member of the group flows through the system of interlocking triangles to touch every person in the system. The system is like a child's mobile. Touching one figure on the mobile automatically affects every other figure on it.

This flow of anxiety explains how groups like churches become polarized and divided. A and B experience a conflict which results in both feeling hurt and angry. The way to move beyond the hurt and anger is for A or B, managing their emotions, to act in a self-differentiated way to address the other. (Compare Matthew 18:15.) But such a response requires courage and emotional-relational-spiritual maturity. An easier, less mature way to deal with the hurt (anxiety) is to share it with another person—to create a triangle. So A goes to C to talk about what happened with B. (We only tell those we believe will sympathize with us, validating our perspective and taking our side.) A and C are in the inside positions of the triangle with B in the outside position. Of course, A tells C his perspective of what B did along with the pain B caused. C is outraged that B would be so inconsiderate as to do such a thing to her friend A. A's anxiety has now stirred C's anxiety. C now carries A's anxiety plus her own. In her outrage, C turns to D to tell D what B did to A. C has engaged another triangle, one that does not directly include A but is connected to A through the interlocking triangles. D too cannot believe B would do such a thing. She shares C's offense, which includes A's original hurt. So now D carries A's and C's anxiety plus her own. The "sharing" will continue, spreading through the various triangles and escalating the anxiety with each sharing.

But of course, A is not the only one talking. B creates her own triangle by talking to her friend X. And like A with C, B tells X her perspective of what happened, including the hurt she experienced at the hand of A. X naturally takes the side of her friend B, now viewing A negatively. X has taken on B's anxiety. True to the nature of interlocking triangles, X will tell Y, who will tell Z. With each retelling, the original anxiety spreads and escalates.

The spread of anxiety continues down both lines until the entire

166

system is infected, resulting in polarization. Everyone is aligned either with A or with B. The division A and B experienced with each other has now spread throughout the larger group. At this level, resolution of the issue will be infinitely more difficult. (How many congregations have experienced this kind of division? How often does it happen?)

Understanding triangles equips us to be an agent of healing and reconciliation in the midst of such dynamics. We recognize the "enlistment" as A or B shares their experience of the conflict. Understanding boundaries, we refuse to buy into the other's anxiety. It is not ours, nor are we responsible for it. It belongs to them. They are responsible for it and alone have power over it. Exercising self-awareness and self-management, we act in a self-differentiated way. We do not get sucked into the spread of the anxiety with its togetherness pressure. We do not take sides. We take a principled "I" position while staying connected with the other. Such a position could be an offer to coach A (or B) in dealing with the alienation in the relationship. It may be to serve as a mediator between the two, seeking to facilitate mutual understanding and reconciliation. The "I" position refuses to take sides. Within the larger group, this act of self-differentiation acts as a circuit breaker that prevents the continuing spread of the anxiety.

Summary

- Triangles grow out of anxiety in the relationship.
- Triangles are an attempt to manage (lower) the anxiety.
- Triangles are an avoidance mechanism, avoiding the risk of being known.
- Triangles create an illusion of intimacy. They create a pseudo intimacy that does not involve the risk of knowing and being known.
- Triangles are invisible in the relationship system. They become apparent when stress and anxiety are high.
- Triangles are the pathway over which the anxiety flows through the relationship system. The level of anxiety builds as it flows through the interlocking triangles.
- Triangles are predictable. They follow predictable rules.

- Efforts to change a triangle or someone in a triangle produce the opposite effect.
- Triangles are resilient. They resist change.
- We can only change a triangle in which we are a direct participant.
- We can only change a triangle by changing how we function in it.

APPENDIX F

Recreating the Land of the Giants:
Thoughts about Parenting

Our experience in the land of the giants leaves a lasting imprint on us. Such imprinting is unavoidable. No child grows up without it. No child leaves the land of the giants without the anxiety of a primary need and dominating fear. The best parenting techniques cannot prevent it. But healthy parenting can diminish the power of the imprint and its anxiety in our child's life. More importantly, healthy parenting will provide a model and training for dealing with the anxiety in a healthy way.

A central component to healthy parenting is our understanding and practice of healthy boundaries. Healthy boundaries help us identify the *goal* of our parenting: to teach our child to be self-responsible while helping them discover their own gifts, abilities, and passions (i.e., their true self).

Training our child to be self-responsible involves training them to focus on themselves rather than on others. We train them to use their power to manage themselves rather than reacting to what others say or do. We train our child to be self-aware, recognizing their emotions. We help them name the emotions. We help them develop a healthy way of expressing them. We teach them how to take care of themselves when they are reacting emotionally rather than dumping their emotion on others. We teach our child to use "I" statements to express what they think, feel, want, and choose.

Training our child to be self-responsible involves helping them learn how to do things for themselves rather than doing things for them. It involves allowing them to do things as best they can without their efforts having to measure up to our expectations. It involves introducing age-appropriate tasks for them to do.

We teach our child about their uniqueness and value. We help them identify and develop their power and innate abilities. We nurture their interests rather than seeking to force them into who we want them to be or what we want them to do. We do not seek to make them over in our image or live our lives through them. We do not use them to bolster our own image, standing, or value. We seek to build their identity around being a beloved child of God.[78]

This goal calls *us* to be self-responsible and to live with healthy boundaries. We are intentional about working on our own issues so that we don't dump them onto our children. We do not dump our frustration and anger, even when they do something to defy us. We understand that having a mind of their own is a part of developing their own identity. When discipline is required, our objective is to teach and train, not to punish. We use natural consequences to teach that their choices have consequences. (Tying consequences to choices is a part of learning to be self-responsible.) When appropriate, we allow them to choose appropriate discipline from a list of options. We avoid any statement or action that demeans or belittles them. We avoid criticizing and judging, ridicule and put-downs. We use "I" statements in our communication, avoiding "you" statements. We use questions to engage their thinking and to understand their thinking. We affirm and encourage. We listen, allowing them to be a part of conversations and decisions.

Perhaps the greatest gift we can give our children is working to grow emotionally-relationally-spiritually. Understanding the four basic emotional needs guides us in how we relate to them. Being a parent is not easy. We will fail. But the more self-responsible we become, the less our issues get passed onto our children. As we work at our own growth and development, we provide them a healthy model for dealing with their own humanness, weaknesses, and failures.

Every child needs a safe place to belong in which who they are and what they can do is valued. Our job as parents is to provide that safe place, guiding their journey of discovering who they are and what they can do.

APPENDIX G

Worried Sick

Worry is a common expression of fear and anxiety. It is primarily rooted in two of our four basic needs: our need to be safe and our need to have a sense of power and ability, to be capable.

We experience worry when we attempt to control something we cannot control. The experience of being powerless in the situation plays on our fear of being incapable and not measuring up. If we are powerless, we are in danger of being hurt. Our sense of being powerless fuels our anxiety.

Worry is always about the future, about what might happen. It is always looking ahead to what might be or could be. This focus on what might be in the future reinforces our sense of powerlessness. It is what keeps worry alive.

When we worry, anxiety and fear have taken control of our hearts and minds. Our minds are frantic, feverishly looking for some way to get in control, to reduce the possibilities down to what we want, to make something happen. Our minds cannot let go of the situation. We obsess about it. Our frantic searching only fuels our sense of powerlessness, which fuels our worry. It creates a self-perpetuating cycle of fear.

We can break free from worry by being self-aware and exercising self-management. We focus our attention back on ourselves and our reactions rather than on the situation. We use our power to manage ourselves and our reactions (the only things over which we have power) rather than attempting to control what we cannot control. We focus on the present, shifting our attention from the future. We release the future into God's sovereignty as we rest in God's peace, love, and faithfulness.

The apostle Paul exhorted his readers to stop worrying (Philippians

4:6–7). His language suggests not giving in to the power of worry. We worry, but we do not have to continue in its grip. Through self-awareness and self-management, we can move beyond its consuming power. Paul exhorted his readers to offset their worry by praying with thanksgiving. Praying places the situation in God's hands. Thanksgiving reminds us of God's faithfulness and blessing in the past. Praying with thanksgiving invites us to remember and to rest in God's faithful love. It places us in a position to experience the peace of Christ that cannot be explained. Peace is the antidote to worry.

APPENDIX H

The Use of Fear in Religious Life

What place does fear have in religious life?

Fear has often been used in religious life as a means of motivation, particularly the fear of retribution and judgment. The prospect of death and the threat of being tortured in hell for eternity have been popular fear-based themes in the preaching of evangelists and well-intentioned pastors. But fear has a limited shelf life as a motivator. While it may produce a decision in the moment, it seldom produces long-lasting change.

Using fear in this way attacks us at a deep, emotional level: the level of our four basic emotional needs. It assaults our need to be safe, playing on our fear of being hurt. It touches our fear of being rejected and abandoned. It plays on our fear of being inadequate and not measuring up. It communicates we are no good and have no value.

Using fear to motivate is a form of manipulation. It plays on our sense of guilt. Almost all of us live with a nebulous feeling of having failed to measure up to some standard of expectations. We know we are weak and we fail. The fear of judgment plays on that awareness. It is particularly powerful when it targets our sense of shame and self-loathing.

The use of fear in religious life is indicative of merit-based thinking. All of the elements of merit-based thinking are there: a standard by which we are judged, acceptance bartered in exchange for conformity, fear of rejection, comparing and competing, *us-them* mentality, *better than-less than* thinking, and self-effort to conform.

The antidote to such manipulation is spiritual growth and maturity, spiritual health and vitality. The writer of Ephesians stated this truth. "We must no longer be children, tossed to and fro and blown about by every wind of doctrine, by people's trickery, by their craftiness in deceitful scheming" (Ephesians 4:14). Living out of spiritual truth frees us from manipulation by fear. The writer of 1 John expressed the same truth. "There is no fear in love, but perfect love casts out fear; for fear has to do with punishment, and whoever fears has not reached perfection in love" (1 John 4:18). Fear is an aspect of merit-based thinking with its rewards and punishments. Love or grace-based thinking moves us beyond fear of punishment. It frees us from being manipulated by fear.

SELECTED BIBLIOGRAPHY

Bowen, Murry. *Family Therapy in Clinical Practice.* Northvale, NJ: Jason Aronson, 1978.

Friedman, Edwin H. *Generation to Generation: Family Process in Church and Synagogue.* New York: The Guilford Press, 1985.

Heifetz, Ronald and Marty Linsky. *Leadership on the Line: Staying Alive through the Dangers of Leading.* Boston, MA: Harvard Business School Press, 2002.

Kerr, Michael. *Bowen Theory's Secrets: Revealing the Hidden Life of Families.* New York: W. W. Norton & Company, 2019.

Langford, Steve. *A God-Shaped World: Exploring Jesus's Teachings about the Kingdom of God and the Implications for the World Today.* Bloomington, IN: WestBow Press, 2017.

_____ *The Fruit of the Spirit: The Path That Leads to Loving as Jesus Loved.* Bloomington, IN: WestBow Press, 2019.

_____ *Why the Bible Is So Hard to Understand … And Tips to Understanding It.* Maitlin, FL: Zulon Press, 2015.

Merton, Thomas. *New Seeds of Contemplation.* New York: New Directions, 2007. (First published in 1962.)

Rohr, Richard. *The Immortal Diamond: The Search for Our True Self.* San Francisco, CA: Jossey-Bass, 2013.

Schwartz, Tony. *The Way We Are Working Isn't Working: The Four Forgotten Needs That Energize Great Performance.* New York: Simon & Schuster, Inc., 2010.

NOTES

Preface

1   I intentionally link emotionally-relationally-spiritually together, using hyphens instead of commas, to communicate that these three areas of growth are interrelated. Growth in one area produces growth in the others.

2   The term *true self* was made popular in the mid-twentieth century by the Trappist monk Thomas Merton. The true self stands in contrast to the false self that Merton referred to as an illusionary person, "the man I want myself to be." (Thomas Merton, *New Seeds of Contemplation*, New York, New York: New Directions, 2007, page 34.) Father Richard Rohr, a Franciscan priest and founder of the Center for Action and Contemplation, described the false self as the ego, a "concocted" self, a small, fragile self that engages in "a game of ego pretend," accessorizes itself by "posturing and pretending," by "climbing, contending, criticizing, and competing." (Richard Rohr, *The Immortal Diamond: The Search for Our True Self*, San Francisco, CA: Jossey-Bass, 2013, page 21.) Rohr described the true self as our own "divine DNA … an *imago Dei* that begs to be allowed, to be fulfilled, and to show itself." (Ibid., page 17.) Those who walk in the mystic circles of Christianity will recognize the term *true self*.
The concept of the true self and false self can also be found in Bowen Family System theory. In his theory about family emotional process, Dr. Murry Bowen spoke of the solid self and the pseudo self. He described the pseudo self as a "pretend self." This pretend self is the self that is shaped by the thinking and emotional pressures of others. It was created by the pressure of family and social groups, what Bowen calls "the relationship system," to conform to their ideals and principles. (Murry Bowen, *Family Therapy in Clinical Practice*, Northvale, New Jersey: Jason Aronson, 1978, page 365.) Bowen's description of the pseudo self aligns with Merton and Rohr's descriptions of the false self. The pseudo self stands in contrast to the solid self, which Bowen described as being made up of clearly defined beliefs, convictions, and life principles based on intellectual reasoning and careful consideration as opposed to the emotional pressures of

different social groups. Those principles guide how the solid self lives. In contrast to Merton and Rohr who tie the true self to God, Bowen ties the solid self to intellectual reasoning.

Chapter 1

3 This concept is expressed in the Serenity Prayer, written by Reinhold Neibuhr (1892–1971) and used widely in recovery groups. "God grant me the serenity to accept the things I cannot change; courage to change the things I can; and wisdom to know the difference."

Chapter 2

4 BFST speaks of acute anxiety and chronic anxiety. Acute anxiety is what I have described as fear—the anxiety related to a present, perceived threat. Chronic anxiety is old anxiety, rooted in past experiences. It is the anxiety we carry inside us. Michael E. Kerr, *Bowen Theory's Secrets: Revealing the Hidden Life of Families* (2019), page 171.

5 Interestingly, uncertainty of the outcome is part of what engages us in sporting events (i.e., going for short yardage on fourth down in football or full count, bases loaded, and tie score in the bottom of the ninth in baseball.)

6 Michael Kerr speaks of a unidisease. By the term he means that underlying the biological processes associated with illness, regardless of the particular illness, is heightened chronic anxiety and anxiety-driven emotional reactivity. Kerr, chapter 23, page 297.

7 BFST refers to these escape strategies as anxiety binders. Ibid., page 25.

8 BFST refers to this focus on a child as the family projection process. Bowen, page. 379.

9 BFST speaks of this pattern as overfunctioning/underfunctioning reciprocity. The overfunctioner takes responsibility for what belongs to another. In doing so, she seeks to control. Overfunctioning allows the other person to underfunction, avoiding the responsibility that belongs to them. Overfunctioning keeps the underfunctioner in a dependent posture. Overfunctioning and underfunctioning complement one another. Kerr, pages 29–31.

10 See appendix G: "Worried Sick."

Chapter 3

11 The story can be found in Mark 5:1–20 as well as in Matthew 8:28–34 and Luke 8:26–39.

12 All scripture quotations are from the New Revised Standard Version, unless otherwise noted. (copyright © 1989 the Division of Christian Education of the National Council of the Churches of Christ in the United States of America. Used by permission.)

13 The word *legion* was the name of a Roman military unit. The number of soldiers in the unit varied between 1,000 and 5,000, depending on the era.

Chapter 4

14 Kerr, pages 71–73.

15 BFST describes this pattern in a relationship as emotional distancing and emotional pursuit. It is a common pattern in every intimate relationship. Ibid., page 43.

16 On page 140 of his book *The Way We Are Working Isn't Working: The Four Forgotten Needs That Energize Great Performance* (2010), Tony Schwartz identifies feeling secure and feeling valued as core needs.

17 Consider how we enjoy helping (a position of strength) but struggle to accept help (a position of weakness (i.e., dependency). This need for power is a prominent part of the aging process. One of the greatest struggles of this particular stage of life is the loss of independence and the increasing sense of dependency.

Chapter 5

18 This portion of the brain is called the amygdala or the reptilian brain.

Chapter 6

19 Notice the *if … then* thinking.

20 Some hear this description as determinative, as though we have no will. The will comes to play when we recognize our patterns and choose to manage them. We exercise the will in order to respond rather than react to a situation, in order to change our pattern. See chapter 19.

Chapter 7

21 Each description attempts to capture the core characteristics of each relational pattern. In real life, traces of other patterns bleed into the dominant pattern. Your own relational pattern is more nuanced than these stripped-down descriptions.

22 All descriptions of individuals are fictitious, created from composite traits associated with each primary need and driving fear.

Chapter 8

23 Emotional boundaries are like fences. They define what is mine and what belongs to the other (ownership), what I am responsible for and what I am not responsible for (responsibility), what I have control over and what I do not (power). Healthy boundaries are a prerequisite for healthy relationships. Assuming responsibility for what another feels and attempting to control what they feel are boundary violations that create unhealthy relationships. Chapter 18 offers a fuller description of relational boundaries.

24 Congregations can live out of this dominant fear. They become conflict avoidant. Their driving purpose is keeping everybody happy. This unspoken policy delegates power to the most emotionally immature who are most likely to be offended and complain. Emotional immaturity rather than spiritual maturity shapes the congregation's culture and sets its agenda.

Chapter 9

25 In BFST, unhealthy togetherness is called emotional fusion or herding. Kerr, page 55.

26 In BFST, this pattern is referred to as emotional cut off. Bowen, page 382.

27 Chicken Little is the central character in an ancient folktale.

28 Couples commonly develop a dance of anger in an effort to resolve their conflict. Each step of the dance is a reaction to what the other person does, rooted in each one's primary fear. (Remember we learned this pattern of focusing on the other in the land of the giants.) Each step is predictable. The dance plays out along these predictable steps, moving toward a repeated resolution in which one person (almost always the same person) gives in in order to end the standoff. The dance (conflict) can be ended early when one person, recognizing the dance, chooses to change their predictable, blaming reaction to a healthier, more self-responsible response. That choice opens the door to resolution.

29 I am indebted to Richard Blackburn and the Lombard Mennonite Peace Center for this concept. The concept is central to the center's Mediation Skills Training Institute for Church Leaders.

Chapter 10

30 Social scientists call this process socialization.

31 Most of our social groups were composed of other, smaller groups or units. These smaller circles were based on factors other than the larger group's standards. Friendships and connections outside of the larger group translated into a circle of friends within the larger group. A family's standing in the larger community often factored in to who was a part of the smaller circles and who was not. Socioeconomic factors, religious affiliation, and ethnic identity were also at play in forming these smaller groups. Personal interests and abilities factored in. For example, a classroom is a social group within the school. Within each class are multiple circles: friends, the popular kids, the new kids, the athletes, the nerds, the cheerleaders, the band kids, etc. Just because a kid was a part of the larger social group (the class) did not automatically translate into being a part of any of the smaller interest-based circles. In family systems, siblings often create groups among themselves: the older kids, the younger kids, the girls, the boys, Mom's kids from her first marriage, Dad's kids from his, etc.

32 At the college I attended, a group of guys who did not pledge a fraternity called themselves "the rejects."

33 This pattern of comparing and judging extends beyond our social groups into the larger society. There it is called scapegoating. Scapegoating is judging a group to be *less than*. The scapegoat is rejected and ostracized. They are judged and condemned. The scapegoat is often portrayed as dangerous or evil. They are identified as the source of problems in society. This way of thinking underlies the high rate of incarceration in American society. In the mid-twentieth century, divorced people suffered as scapegoats. The stigma associated with divorce gradually dissipated as divorce became more common. Until the civil rights movement, African Americans played this role. Their role as a scapegoat was reflected in the "N" word by which they were called. Any minority group can be scapegoated, such as Latinos/as, Muslims, members of the LGBTQ+ community, and immigrants. Whether in personal relationships, in social groups, or in the larger society, judging others as *less than* allows us to feel good about ourselves at the other's expense. Scapegoating is a window into our shadow self.

34 See appendix C: "Symptoms of the Constructed Self Syndrome in Religious Life."

Chapter 12

35 Recovery programs, such as AA and Al Anon, demonstrate that peace, progress, personal growth, and authentic relationships are found in honestly acknowledging and dealing with our shadow. It is a counterculture way of being and living.

36 In their book *Leadership on the Line: Staying Alive through the Dangers of Leading*, Ronald Heifetz and Marty Linsky spoke of emotional hungers and their power to disrupt effective leadership. They identified three primary hungers: power and control, affirmation and importance, and intimacy and delight. Ronald Heifetz and Marty Linsky, *Leadership on the Line: Staying Alive through the Dangers of Leading* (Harvard Business School Press, 2002), page 164. These three hungers align with the four basic needs: power and control relate to the need for power, affirmation and importance relate to the need for value, intimacy and delight relate to the need for belonging.

Chapter 13

37 The Greek word Paul used is the word from which we get the English word *metamorphosis*.

Chapter 14

38 This truth goes against the common belief that we are inherently sinful (original sin, total depravity). Could it be our problem is not with how we were created but with how we learned to live? Merit-based thinking leads us to reject our humanness with its limitations and in-process nature. We view others through the lens of fear. We hide from them, only presenting what we believe is acceptable. A fear-based competitive spirit governs our relationships. We abandon the God kind of life for which we were created, exchanging it for an appearance-based existence that leaves us immature and empty.

39 Also see Ephesians 1:3–5.

40 The ways of the kingdom are the focus of my book *A God-Shaped World: Exploring the Teachings of Jesus about the Kingdom of God and the Implications for the Church Today* (WestBow, 2017).

41 See Acts 2 for a description of the outpouring of the Spirit on men and women, young and old.

42 Also see Ephesians 4:13, "to maturity, to the measure of the full stature of Christ," and Romans 8:28–29, "conformed to the image of his Son."

43 See 1 Corinthians 12–14 for the full context. Also see Romans 12:4–8; Ephesians 4:7, 11–16; and 1 Peter 4:10–11.

Chapter 15

44 The character of God is described more fully in my book *A God-Shaped World: Exploring the Teachings of Jesus about the Kingdom of God and the Implications for the Church Today* (WestBow, 2017).
45 See John 1:14, 16; Colossians 1:15 and 19; and Hebrews 1:1–3.
46 See Mark 10:41–45 and Philippians 2:5–11.
47 See Matthew 5:43–48.
48 The description of God's character in Exodus 34:6–7 states that God abounds in faithful love, extending to the thousandth generation, meaning forever.
49 "You have stripped off the old self with its practices and have clothed yourselves with the new self, which is *being renewed in knowledge according to the image of its creator*" (Colossians 3:9–10; emphasis added). Also see Philippians 1:6.
50 "And we know that in all things God works for the good of those who love him, who have been called according to his purpose. For those God foreknew he also predestined to be conformed to the image of his Son, that he might be the firstborn among many brothers and sisters" (Romans 8:28–29 NIV).
51 See appendix D: "Grace-Based versus Merit-Based Religious Life."

Chapter 16

52 See Galatians 3:26–28 and Colossians 3:9–11, where all social distinctions are set aside in Christ.
53 The fruit of the Spirit includes five relational terms: patience, kindness, generosity, faithfulness, and gentleness. The five relational traits are how love is expressed in a relationship as the Spirit empowers us. For a more detailed treatment of Paul's teaching in Galatians 5:21–22, see my book *The Fruit of the Spirit: The Path That Leads to Loving as Jesus Loved* (WestBow, 2019).

Chapter 17

54 The fragile nature of the constructed, ego-based self reminds me of Jesus's parable about the man who built his house upon sand (Matthew 7:24–27).
55 See John 14:27 and Philippians 4:6–7.
56 See again Romans 8:28–29 along with 2 Corinthians 1:3–4 and James 1:2–4.

57 The question "How much is enough?" is seldom asked. When the question is asked, the answer is simple. "Just a little more than I have!"

58 See Jesus's warning against the insatiable desire for more (greed) in Luke 12:13–21.

59 See 2 Corinthians 9:6–8.

Chapter 18

60 The thinking presented here is more fully developed in chapter 6 of my book *The Fruit of the Spirit: The Path That Leads to Loving as Jesus Loved* (WestBow, 2019.)

61 Edwin Friedan, *Generation to Generation: Family Process in Church and Synagogue* (1985), page 27. Also Bowen, page 362, and Kerr, chapter 5, page 46.

Chapter 20

62 BFST compares this functioning to a step-down transformer that reduces the voltage of electricity passing through it. These transformers work between powerlines and homes, reducing the high-voltage electricity of the powerlines to a 110 voltage, which is safe for consumer use. When we are reactive, we function as a step-up transformer that increases the voltage of the anxiety.

Chapter 23

63 See again chapter 14: "Stinking Thinking about Self."

64 This concept of giving out of our journey to help another is expressed in the final step of the twelve-step program.

Chapter 24

65 In BFST, bridges are known as triangles. As the solution to our emotional bind and the answer to our relational dilemma, triangles are the basic building blocks of relationships. See appendix E: "Triangles: The Geometry of Relationships."

66 Other sources identify four to seven levels. These six are adapted from the work of Gary Smalley.

67 We see this reality on Facebook as friends unfriend one another over political differences.

Chapter 25

68 The five relational traits identified in the fruit of the Spirit.
69 See again chapters 19 and 20.

Chapter 26

70 Some interpreters see Paul's words as reference to the Second Coming of Jesus the Messiah, assuring his readers of Christ's ultimate triumph over sin and death, including the challenges they were facing.
71 See Philippians 3:8–11.
72 The pattern of death and resurrection is reflected in the three components of a growth experience: from, into, and by means of.

Chapter 27

73 The anxiety of the organization or workplace can be easily identified. Every group has policies and procedures designed to create stability and smooth functioning. Such policies and procedures are the codified expectations of the group. They are used to ensure conformity and, thereby, manage the anxiety. Every group struggles with progress and change, additional evidence of the anxiety that exists within it. The level of stress in the system is a gauge reflecting the level of anxiety within it at any given time. No group is exempt from the conflict and chaos that occur when the anxiety is triggered.

Appendix A

74 Denise is a colleague and friend who is on her own journey of emotional-relational-spiritual growth. Her story is an example of how old, anxiety-driven patterns surface in our adult lives, sabotaging our lives today. It is also an example of self-awareness and self-management. Her story is used with written permission.

Appendix B

75 Gail is a member of one of the congregations I served and is spiritual friend. Her husband, also my friend, died in January 2019. She was diagnosed with stage 4

metastasized breast cancer in January 2020. This writing is a journal entry in which she relates a frightening dream that woke her. It reflects her self-awareness and ability to center herself in God's peace, displacing her fear and anxiety. Her story is used with written permission.

76 Quoted from The Message by Eugene Peterson. Copyright © 2002. Used by permission of Tyndale House Publishers, a division of Tyndale House Ministries. All rights reserved.

Appendix C

77 This material was first published on my blogsite on September 1, 2019. My blogs are available at pastorstevelangford.blogspot.com or through my web site, pastorstevelangford.com.

Appendix F

78 I am indebted to Rev. Dr. Leanne Hadley, United Methodist elder, for a blessing I use with children. Drawing a cross on the back of their hand with my finger, I say, "You are a beloved child of God." Drawing a circle around the cross, I say, "And God's love will always surround you." Then, turning the child's hand over so the palm is facing up, I place my palm on their palm and say, "And because you are God's child, God will use your hands to be a blessing to others."